The HAPPY Staffordshire Bull Terrier

Raise a Happy, Well-Mannered Dog and Avoid Dog Behaviour Professionals for Life

- Happiness Tips
- Techniques for a Well-behaved Staffordshire Bull Terrier
- Prevent Behaviour Issues
- Fulfil Your Puppy's Needs
- Be the Ideal Guardian
- Avoid Common Mistakes

Asia Moore

Dog Behaviour Expert & Acclaimed Author

Author: Asia Moore
www.K-9SuperHeroesDogWhispering.com
www.KnowsToNose.com
www.MustHavePublishing.com
www.AskBoris.com

Editor & Researcher: Alex Warrington, Ph.D.

Published by:
Worldwide Information Publishing
London
Great Britain
2021

DOGS NEVER LIE ABOUT LOVE

"Dogs are small rays of light caught on the Earth a short time to brighten our days."
— Unknown

Preface

It takes commitment, consistency, time, tenacity, knowledge and firm, vigilant energy to raise a happy and healthy Staffordshire Bull Terrier that doesn't suffer from behavioural or stress-related health issues.

This book is different from most other breed-specific books, because we believe that it's far better for all parties concerned (human and canine) to **prevent** problems rather than suffering the frustrations of living with or learning how to eliminate problems and rehabilitate a Staffordshire Bull Terrier that has already developed health or unwanted behavioural issues.

Of course, it's always better to prevent unwanted behaviours, rather than to hope that you, or someone else, may have what it takes to eliminate them sometime in the future, after your dog has been deemed aggressive or dangerous, your neighbours hate you, your friends no longer visit, your family is at their wits end, and you're having guilty thoughts of re-homing every time you drive past your local SPCA.

FACT ***If you want a happy, well-mannered canine companion to be a loyal, well-behaved and valued member of your family, it absolutely DOES matter how you raise your dog and if you have the right energy for the particular dog you have chosen.***

Every breed has uniquely different talents and needs. Even those that were once primarily bred to be working dogs (such as the Staffordshire Bull Terrier) that have now become companion breeds.

As an example, the Border Collie is a very smart, high-energy working dog that excels at the job of herding. Therefore, if you expect this dog to sit around doing nothing all day while you're at work, you will most likely return to ripped up baseboards, chewed up carpets and a once tidy home that looks like it's been torn apart by a gang of thieves.

On the other hand, the Shih Tzu lap dog, that was originally only permitted to be owned by the wealthy aristocracy, sat on elegant silk pillows, and was used to warm beds and provide comfort, has vastly different daily exercise requirements, and would be a poor choice for someone whose lifestyle called for a canine companion that could protect them from being assaulted by rioters on streets ravaged by marauding gangs.

The bold and sturdy Staffordshire Bull Terrier that was primarily bred to be a vermin catcher and courageous pit fighter, is now a furry companion for many humans.

FACT ***While the Staffordshire Bull Terrier type of dog has a reputation for being dangerous and one of the "Pit Bull" types of dog that is banned from many cities and even entire countries, when properly trained and socialised, they can be friendly and loving companions.***

Sadly, many ignorant, irresponsible dog owners get this tough looking type of dog, never socialise or teach it anything, seriously neglect it, and leave him or her tied up in the back yard to display a scary looking guard dog to passers-by.

When you think about it, who is really to blame if this type of dog retains aggressive tendencies? The creation of blood sports and fighting dogs can be traced back to the Roman Empire. We humans created several breeds to be especially courageous (including the Staffordshire), so that they could be used for gambling entertainment. These tenacious dogs would not hesitate to fight each other to the death in pits, and even though pit fighting has been banned for many years, illegal fighting rings still exist.

FACT ***Pit fighting dogs were specifically bred for "gameness" (to ignore injury or the threat of injury) when facing their opponents, while being loyal and affectionate with their humans.***

In order to raise a happy and healthy Staffordshire fur friend, you need to be totally honest with yourself and absolutely certain that you have the lifestyle and strong energy needed to properly train, socialise and responsibly care for this robust canine companion.

When choosing this dog for your companion, keep in mind that many people may avoid you or treat you and your fur friend with unfair prejudice because of all the negative press surrounding this type of breed.

In a best-case situation, with a well-bred dog and a guardian who does everything right, you can expect the Staffordshire Bull Terrier to be an athletic, agile, loyal, dependable and good-natured companion that will be devoted, gentle and loving with their family.

In an imperfect world, this strong willed, powerful and muscular dog may quickly revert to their fighting ancestry if they feel at all challenged or confronted by a dominant dog that gets up in their face or displays any sort of confrontational energy.

When considering sharing your life with this breed, conscientious guardians need to fully understand and recognize that if anything goes wrong along the way, either with the initial breeding program, inadequate socialising, training or ongoing management by a guardian who understands how important their role will be in the proper raising of this dog, problems may occur.

For instance, while the Staffy is usually non-aggressive with people, should their prey instinct suddenly flare up, this strong dog is entirely capable of seriously harming or killing other animals, such as the neighbour's pedigreed cat, or your child's beloved guinea pig.

DID YOU KNOW? ***This is a confident and fearless dog that often has a strong mind of their own. While they may get along fine with other well-mannered dogs, there's certainly no guarantee that this tenacious Terrier won't decide to take on a much larger dog, such as Doberman or Rottweiler if he or she feels challenged.***

While the Staffordshire Bull Terrier can have a widely varied response to interaction with unknown humans that may vary from polite and quiet indifference to exuberant jumping and friendly face licking, this is a dog that will often display aggression toward unknown dogs. This means that unless you have worked diligently to curb these tendencies, you and your dog will most likely not be very welcome in any dog parks or at any off leash social gatherings.

While strangers will usually be greeted in a friendly manner, this may not be the case with their dogs and it will be important that you are a firm leader that understands how to keep this dog under firm control.

As well, while some of these Terriers have very little guarding instinct, others may have a naturally strong guarding instinct. If you permit a dog with a strong guarding instinct to believe that they must protect you, as they become adults, they will very likely display aggression toward strangers, and this may put both of you in a dangerous situation.

This is a strong, powerful and agile dog that will appreciate an activity-filled lifestyle that involves running, hiking, biking or participating in endless canine sports with their family. He or she may be the perfect companion for a family with someone who works at home, is retired, so long as they are firm and consistent with rules and boundaries so that this dog never questions that you are the boss.

TIP ***This dog will almost certainly become overweight if they do not receive adequate vigorous daily exercise. Most Staffordshires are sturdy, energetic dogs that need regular daily exercise to maintain the correct weight.***

Every dog breed has different talents and needs and when you decide to share your life with a particular breed, if you want a happy and well-adjusted companion, you must also be prepared to provide your dog with what he or she needs to be a safe and happy member of your family.

Almost all canine problems, both mentally and physically, are a direct result of mismatched energy levels, lack of leadership, knowledge, time or unwillingness on the part of the human guardian to choose the right dog for their particular energy and lifestyle. It takes research, time and commitment to learn what each dog truly needs.

This book is uniquely different, and humans reading it need to clearly understand that the pages of this book are not all about describing what to do to eliminate problematic canine behaviours that have already occurred.

Rather, the main focus of this breed-specific book is to describe what the human guardian needs to understand and commit to doing on a daily basis in order to match the Staffordshire Bull Terrier 's needs, so that they can raise a happy, healthy and well-behaved dog that never has to experience behavioural issues.

FACT ***The sturdy and courageous Staffordshire is an especially tenacious and often intimidating Terrier, which means you MUST be in control of their actions at all times, especially if you want to keep peace with the neighbours.***

Do not expect this book to be like all the others that set out endless correlations between specific mal-behaviours and various steps or actions the human guardian can take in an attempt to correct them.

In other words, this book is a totally new slant on raising a happy and healthy Staffordshire Bull Terrier, because the main focus here is on the prevention of behavioural issues rather than addressing them after they have already surfaced.

"Dogs make humans feel special."

~Asia Moore~

About the Author

Asia Moore

Dog Behaviour Expert & Acclaimed Author

Ever since my first birthday, I was immersed in nature, and have always enjoyed a special connection with all creatures, both great and small. I learned to communicate and "talk" with many animals in their language, both wild and domesticated. At approximately the age of twelve, dogs began to become the main focus of my life, when I set about training and grooming my first puppy.

When friends and neighbours began to recognize how well behaved my dog was, and were subsequently impressed with all the tricks and routines she could perform, often without a spoken word, they asked me to train their dogs, too.

I count myself very fortunate to have experienced the unconditional love of so many dogs, all of who taught me many different life lessons. I began this journey with my first Setter/Spaniel mixed breed ("Cindy") who protected me from my marauding brothers, then my Cocker Spaniel/Poodle/Terrier/Sheltie mixed breed ("Pepper") who had an amazing human vocabulary and always knew when someone was not to be trusted, my Jack Russell Terrier ("Juno") whose tenacious antics made me laugh every day, my Blue Heeler ("Bugsy") who would hike endless trails and swim miles with me, to my wise and loving Shih Tzu ("Boris") and all my clients' dogs in between.

A frolicking cascade of amazing fur friends that includes endless different pure breeds, and many hybrids and mutts, from tiny Chihuahuas to bouncing Belgians, has passed through my life.

This also includes spending a considerable amount of time with a loving Staffordshire Bull Terrier named *"Arturo",* whom I used to dog sit for many years.

I have been managing my dog whispering, dog sitting and matchmaking businesses over the past 40 years and have enjoyed countless experiences working with dogs of all breeds and their guardians. While life may sometimes bring us challenges and setbacks, I've never stopped learning from the many dogs that have graced my life, and I've always been passionate about what I do.

Countless years of experience taught me invaluable lessons in all aspects of the human-canine relationship interaction. For instance, I learned how to effectively communicate with our canine friends, understand their needs and help them and their human guardians lead an enjoyable and blessed life together. *What could be better than that?*

While clients' dogs remain the centre of my dog whispering, and dog sitting life, I also focus on writing books with a goal to pass on my knowledge and experience to all responsible dog people (**Must Have Publishing.com**). At the same time, I continue to educate human guardians, so that they can improve relationships with their dogs and understand how to prevent and alleviate behavioural issues (**K-9 Super Heroes Dog Whispering.com**). My husband and I are also working on bringing smiles to humans at the website dedicated to our dear Boris, where you will soon be able to find memes, sayings, pictures, "talking" dogs, educational articles, how to easily find excellent products every dog needs, and more. (**AskBoris.com**).

Also, I have an online matchmaking service **(Knows To Nose.com)** to help humans *"know"* how to choose the right dog *"nose"* for their energy and lifestyle, before they make the wrong decision and end up with troubling problems.

I am also often called upon to speak to groups about the changing roles of the canine population and how working breeds can find new ways to fit into our modern world. As well, I help humans and their chosen canines establish harmonious relationships between neighbours for those residing in multi-family living situations, such as apartment and condominium complexes.

I am so fortunate that the canine world has been such a large part of my life for so many years, as it never gets old, and with every new dog there's always an opportunity to learn something new. I continuously stay in touch with my clients through my business websites and personal consultations and I love how every unique dog/human relationship brings new lessons to light and enhances everyone's life in untold, indescribable ways.

*I'd like to thank you for purchasing "**The Happy Staffordshire Bull Terrier**" book and reassure you that these pages contain the distilled knowledge of over 40 years experience, which, by the way, includes helping a nervous dog suffering from anxiety about crossing over unfamiliar, slippery floor tiles.*

When taken to heart, the knowledge, tips and techniques in this book can help you along your special journey inside the amazing world of our canine friends, so that you can know the unconditional love, special bond and joy that only our four-legged companions selflessly offer to us flawed humans.

Visit Asia online at the following .com locations:

www.K-9SuperHeroesDogWhispering.com
www.KnowsToNose.com
www.MustHavePublishing.com
www.AskBoris.com

Table of Contents

Chapter 1: Introduction

"Properly trained, a man can be dog's best friend."
— Corey Ford

The purpose of this book is to focus on the essential steps the people in this relationship truly need to be aware of and commit to providing in order to ensure that this powerful and imposing Terrier can live a happy and healthy life, which in turn will ensure a harmonious relationship for everyone.

Despite the fact that humans and dogs have been depending on one another for more than 30,000 years, it's still highly important that you take an honest look at your life, to decide whether sharing your life with a dog is truly feasible, and then if it is, choose the fur comrade that is best suited to your particular energy and lifestyle.

Within the pages of this book, you will find tips, facts and information to help you choose wisely by providing you with a clear understanding concerning whether or not YOU have the right energy for raising a happy and well-mannered Staffordshire Bull Terrier companion.

In addition, this book describes in detail what the human guardian needs to keep in mind and commit to doing on a daily basis in order to match this bright, energetic and highly trainable companion's needs, so that they can raise a happy, healthy and well-behaved dog that never has to experience behavioural issues.

All the information, suggestions, tips and advice given in this publication is the result of more than 40 years' experience helping humans positively and effectively interact with the canine world.

If you take all that is written on these pages to heart, and regularly and routinely apply them, your active, and loyal Staffordshire will be a happy family member that will not have to suffer from any behavioural problems. In other words, this book places the **focus on prevention**, rather than attempting to correct troublesome issues after they have surfaced.

Every Chapter of this book contains valuable information that will provide you with a concrete understanding of the breed and what's involved in raising a happy and well-behaved companion.

For instance, **Chapter 2** – *"Asia's Happiness Tips"* sets out a summary of what she personally believes makes for a happy Staffordshire Bull Terrier and encourages you to ask yourself what YOU think would make this dog happy.

Chapter 3 – "*Overview of the Happy Staffordshire Bull Terrier*" will outline vital statistics, coat colours and common features, intelligence, temperament and interesting secrets and facts that may not be commonly known.

Further, in order to raise a contented dog, it's important to have some basic knowledge of the interesting history of the Staffordshire breed, so that you are able to better comprehend this dog's needs.

Chapter 4 – *"Healthy Staffordshire Bull Terrier = Happy Dog"* is where you will find out what you need to know about medical care, safety and health issues that may affect this small-sized breed, including common diseases and viruses, allergies and canine CPR procedures that could save a life. Needless to say, if your dog is not physically healthy, he or she will not be a happy canine companion for very long, because suffering from health-related issues will undoubtedly create a miserable and ill-mannered dog.

In **Chapter 5** – *"Let Your Dog BE a Happy Dog"*, you will find information about how to let your Staffordshire actually BE a dog, rather than attempting to turn them into a fur human, which can make for a very confused, unhappy and ill-mannered canine.

Chapter 6 –*"Every Happy Staffordshire Bull Terrier Wants Exercise"*, first outlines some of the original history of this dog when they were originally created as working vermin exterminators and pit fighters that have become more of a companion.

When you are aware of what they were originally bred to do, you will better understand how important it is to commit to the daily exercise routines recommended in this book, without which this Terrier will not be happy or healthy for very long.

Chapter 7 – *"Feeding the Happy Staffordshire Bull Terrier"* is where you will find information about the various food options and feeding suggestions as well as treats to avoid that will assist you in raising a happy and healthy companion.

In **Chapter 8** – *"Care of the Happy Staffordshire Bull Terrier",* you will find travel safety tips, licensing, insurance, essential grooming procedures and important care of nails, ears, teeth and paws, all of which will help you to raise a happy and healthy dog.

While some of this information might seem universal, imagine how you might feel functioning for months without washing your hair, cutting your nails or brushing your teeth. Regrettably, that is the actuality for many dogs, due to their owners not having been accurately advised with respect to the importance of good grooming habits. How happy and well behaved do you think such a poorly cared for dog would be?

Chapter 9 – *"Are YOU the Ideal Happy Staffordshire Bull Terrier Guardian?"* is concerned with asking yourself some serious questions, as well as whether your energy, activity, commitment and lifestyle matches what this sturdy dog needs to be happy and well behaved. It's vital for you to give thoughtful consideration to these questions when considering any breed, because should you choose the wrong dog to share your life with, everybody will suffer the consequences.

Chapter 10 – *"Humans Can Make Mistakes"* outlines that far too often we humans, without even realizing it, are the cause of creating behavioural problems in our canine companions. Here you will read about some of the common oversights to avoid (and the right thing to do!) when it comes to socialisation, accidental rewards, fear of noises, the right collars, basic rules and boundaries, adolescent craziness and more.

TIP ***Simply being aware of the many blunders, we humans can often inadvertently be guilty of when raising our canine companions,***

can mean the difference between a Happy Staffordshire Bull Terrier with no behavioural issues or a life of frustration and correction.

Chapter 11 – *"Happy Staffordshire Bull Terrier Body Language"*, outlines the foundation of learning canine body language, and will help you be more aware of what's going on around other dogs. Learning to properly "read" a dog's intentions can prevent an unwanted encounter with another dog or human, and this will help everyone to remain safe and happy.

In Chapter 12 – *"Training Basics for a Happy Staffordshire Bull Terrier"*, you will learn valuable training tips and routines that will help to keep your dog truly happy and well behaved for their entire life. It's no surprise that a well-trained dog will be a much happier companion that everyone enjoys being around, and that will be far less likely to develop behaviour issues somewhere down the road.

Developing a basic training program and learning to teach your dog commands and discipline that establishes a strong bond of trust and respect between human and canine is all part of starting your dog off on the right paw.

Chapter 13 – *"What If You Slip Up?"* is only necessary because we humans tend to get too engrossed and overwhelmed with the rigors of daily living, which means we sometimes forget to be consistent with providing what our particular dog may need to be happy. If you slip up, this Chapter has outlined a few of the more common behavioural issues and how to promptly get yourself back on track.

Chapter 14 – *"Surprise Bonus Chapter"* is a Question & Answer section containing a few human/canine scenarios with humans asking questions and wise words from the perspective of the dog, who will answer the questions. You will also find a humorous and educational true story about a stubborn dog that refused to set one paw on the newly installed tiles in his family home.

Take heed humans, because when you honestly assess your own abilities, compatibility, lifestyle and energy level for being the right guardian for the faithful Staffordshire Bull Terrier, and are vigilant about following the advice and tips outlined in the following pages, you can raise a healthy and happy dog that will be a joy to live with and will never have to suffer from any behavioural issues.

Chapter 2: Asia's Happiness Tips

"Dogs do speak, but only to those who know how to listen."
— Orhan Pamuk

The following few paragraphs are a summary of my own personal ramblings, ideas and beliefs about what I think makes for a happy and contented Staffordshire Bull Terrier.

While I hope you may wholeheartedly agree, it's absolutely fine if you have other ideas, or if you may have an entirely different take on this subject, because while we may all have our own "personal" ideas about what might make a Staffordshire happy, if your ideas are different from mine, this does not mean that they are any less valid.

If you're considering sharing your life with this confident and often willful canine and have never before really sat down and consciously thought about what would make this particular breed truly happy, while you may gain a little insight from reading about my own personal beliefs, I encourage you to take the time to carry out this exercise yourself. If you have a family, get them involved in this fun exercise, too.

When you take the time to sit with a piece of paper and pen and begin to write down what YOU think would make this dog happy, you may be surprised about what surfaces, and this simple exercise may inspire you and your family to discover new ways to bond with your dog, which will be the basis of having a truly happy relationship.

I'll help to get you started with the following question:
"What do you think would make a Staffordshire Bull Terrier happy?"

I've shared the last 15 years of my life with a wonderfully loving and well-behaved Shih Tzu and I believe that the very best start you can make, with respect to "happiness" when first bringing home your new puppy is to do all you can to reassure him or her that they are not alone (see below).

Happy New Surroundings

The puppy will be understandably nervous about the new and unfamiliar faces, smells and surroundings, and will understandably be missing their mother, other siblings and everything in their environment they had grown used to during their first 8 to 10 weeks of life.

Make sure that you don't overwhelm your new puppy with too much all at once. For instance, close off rooms that you don't need access to and encourage your puppy to come to you as you wander about in a smaller space.

Happy Sleep Patterns

When it's time to go to bed, take your puppy outside for a bathroom break, and then make sure that you have a nice, cozy kennel all ready for your new puppy with a soft lining or blanket, a toy and a treat and place their new kennel inside your bedroom, so that they will be able to hear and see you.

TIP ***Unless you want your sturdy Staffy to sleep on your bed when they're fully grown, even when they may have wet or dirty feet, or just rolled in a dead rat, now is the time to exercise a little tough love as the new puppy will most likely not want to be alone in their kennel and will prefer sleeping next to you.***

If your bed is large enough to accommodate their kennel, this is the best way to help your puppy have a happy sleep time because they will be next to you, but still safe inside their own kennel, and as they grow larger, they will be used to their kennel and will not mind that it is sitting on the floor. Congratulations! You've just created a routine that will ensure happy and respectful sleeping patterns for your dog.

Happy Puppy Play

Taking the time for regular play sessions with your new Terrier puppy will certainly make them very happy, so make sure you set aside several times during your day when you stop with the human work and chores and engage your puppy in fun games for 5 or 10 minutes at least three or four times a day.

TIP ***Never let this puppy win when you're playing a tug game, because you want to establish early on (before they are overly strong) that you are the boss and they must always accede to your will.***

Happy Puppy Housetraining

One of the very first things your new puppy needs to learn is where the bathroom is, and the more observant and watchful you are, the fewer "accidents" will occur, which will make both of you much happier.

I taught my Shih Tzu (Boris) to ring a little bell whenever he needed to go outside, which is a very valuable "trick" to teach. Just hang a loud ringing bell at the end of a ribbon, string or rope from the doorknob of the door (or next to it) where you will always take your dog to go outside for a bathroom break. Every time you take them out, go to the bell, lift their paw and knock it against the bell to make it ring. Say *"Good boy, or girl – go pee?"* Then immediately take them out through this door.

When you learn to pay attention, be observant and understand your dog's body language, you can help teach them proper bathroom habits at a very young age. This is an intelligent dog that wants to please and it should not be difficult to quickly train them that outside is where they need to go to get to their bathroom.

When they wake up in the morning, take them outside immediately. Twenty minutes after they have eaten a meal, take them outside to relieve themselves. After a play session or when they've had a big drink of water, or woken up from a nap, take them outside. After they've gone pee or number 2, immediately praise and reward them with a treat.

Yes, to do this correctly, you and your puppy will be spending a lot of time going outside together, but once their bladder grows larger and stronger, the number of hours he or she can "hold" it will increase, and the number of times your dog will have to visit the great outdoor bathroom during each day will become less.

Take advantage of this bathroom training time, as it can be a way to create a strong bond between you and your dog and as their first lessons in leash and reward training for doing what you ask and being an obedient follower.

TIP ***When you go out with them while they're on leash, it's easy to train your dog to "go" on command, and as they mature, you'll***

be very glad that you took the time to do this, especially if you live in a climate that has cold or wet winters.

Happy Puppy Feeding

We all know that providing your puppy or dog with the best nutrition from the very first day you bring them home will produce a healthier fur friend, which in turn, will lead to a feel-good, energetic and happy companion.

Be aware of the consequences of what you feed your dog and commit to doing the best you can to keep your canine friend healthy and happy. Read labels and feed them only the highest-quality food, so they have the best opportunity for a long life.

While it's important to start your puppy off with the right food, it's just as important to continue to feed your adult dog the very best diet. Please refer to Chapter 7 (Feeding the Happy Staffordshire Bull Terrier), where you will read about types of food, appropriate treats and more.

Happy Socialising

Socialising a new puppy is one of the most important steps you can take to ensure that your chosen companion lives a happy and stress-free life.

When you don't take the time to properly socialise your puppy, and indeed, keep on socialising throughout their lifetime, you can actually create many behavioural issues, some of which can be so severe that your dog may be in danger of having their life prematurely shortened.

For instance, the Staffordshire Bull Terrier already has it in him or her to be a confident, dominant and often confrontational character that has a willful mind of his or her own and possibly a strong prey drive. If you pair this up with a mild-mannered human guardian that does not recognize the importance of providing proper socialising and firm rules and boundaries, so that this dog becomes a calm follower, he or she may quickly take over, which could get both of you into much trouble.

Many times, I've been called upon to help a human alleviate aggressive tendencies being displayed by their canine companion, and in pretty much every instance, this could have been entirely avoided if firm rules and boundaries had been established early on and the dog had been properly trained and socialised from the get go.

In the case of the Staffordshire, if you make the mistake of coddling and babying this determined companion and allowing him or her to be in control, you can end up creating a dominant, aggressive dog that is downright disagreeable, with a reputation for being a cat killer or an aggressive dog everyone should avoid at all costs.

Every dog must have a human leader to keep them safe and teach them appropriate rules and boundaries, and some dogs, such as the Staffy, require a stronger lead from their human counterparts. Most dogs also require a significant amount of socialising, and more daily exercise and mental stimulation than you might imagine.

FACT ***If you socialise well and keep this dog exercised and tired out every day, there will be much less chance of a confrontational encounter with unknown dogs.***

The Staffordshire will need to be well and continually socialised at a young age, and taught to keep their enthusiasm or any tendency to dominate under control. They will be interested participants that enjoy being involved in all of the family's activities, especially if they involve hiking, running, swimming, learning tricks, a canine sport, or plenty of varied outdoor adventures.

reminder ***When not properly socialised, trained and taught to respect the word of their human guardians, this powerful and determined companion may soon become a bossy leader if their human's energy is not strong enough for this dog to respectfully follow.***

Without a human to trust, respect and follow, any dog can get themselves and their humans into all sorts of unwanted troubles. Often, dogs that do not have a human to lead them can feel forced into acting out in an aggressive manner.

Keep in mind that the tenacious and fearless Staffordshire is not normally timid or shy, but rather quite naturally confident and will easily fall into the leadership role, which can lead to aggressive behaviour. You definitely do not want this muscular and powerful dog to act out on his or her own.

Any sort of aggression is a huge stress on both dog and human and, as we are all aware, stress shortens lives and prevents anyone from experiencing happiness. Help make your dog happy by being a strong and confident leader for him or her, rather than allowing the very heavy burden of making human decisions to be placed on the shoulders of your best fur friend.

While early socialisation of a puppy is very important, keep in mind that it's just as important to continue a grown dog's socialisation throughout the course of his or her entire lifetime. Please refer to Chapter 10 (Humans Can Make Mistakes) that outlines the many aspects of socialising your Staffordshire.

Happy Training

Almost as important as proper socialising for helping to keep your dog safe and happy, is proper training, which should never be overlooked, unless you want to create a dominant, unstable Terrier that ignores their humans, barks, displays aggression, and thinks they are the boss of all they survey.

Eager to please, highly trainable, playful and amusing, this feisty character approaches life with a keenly alert sense of fun and adventure, while eager to chase anything that moves. This is a small dog with a large enthusiasm and zest for life. A calm, structured living situation that ensures a regular, vigorous exercise routine will prevent anxiety and other behavioural problems that may stem from being under-challenged.

With the right guardian, this determined Terrier could easily become a top performer in the trick training arena and many other popular canine sports. In order to maintain their health, regular daily exercise and learning interesting routines will prevent their tendency to become overweight, which can lead to problem health issues.

This confident, muscular Terrier may retain a strong prey drive that means they may not recognize the innocent neighbour's cat as anything more than vermin to be immediately eliminated.

Depending on how curious they may be, how much exercise they normally receive outside of the home, and how strong their prey drive, when not properly trained, this dog may ignore calls to come back when they are on the scent of something interesting.

It can be very difficult, if not impossible, to train the prey drive out of this Terrier that has been strictly bred for killing vermin and pit fighting since the early 1800s.

Start training this companion as soon as you bring him or her home from the breeder and you will have given yourself the best opportunity to have a happy, eager to comply and safe companion at your side before they are six months old. Of course, you will start out with short training sessions of no more than 5 to 10 minutes at a time, and as they slowly mature, you can increase the length of your sessions.

Make sure any training is a fun and happy time for both you and your dog, with lots of happy praise and treats, and he or she will quickly learn to trust and respect you as their leader and be eager for their next session. This loyal, energetic Terrier is loving and friendly with their human family and will be an easy to train dog that should catch on very quickly.

While this smart puppy can begin training at an early age, when you continue their training throughout their life, this companion will usually be an eager participant that is entirely capable of learning many commands, tricks, routines, and hand signals, as well as several canine sports. See more in Chapter 12 (Training Basics for a Happy Staffordshire Bull Terrier).

The Staffy is a strong, powerful and agile dog that will appreciate an activity-filled lifestyle that involves biking, hiking, running or participating in canine sports and outdoor activities with their human family.

FACT ***If this dog escapes the home or yard, they may entertain themselves by hunting vermin or chasing the neighbour's cat.***

Happy Exercising

While the Staffordshire Bull Terrier is intelligent and versatile, and they enjoy learning new routines, they also need some down time, or some time off from your vigilant supervision.

FACT ***Just like us humans, who need time where they don't have to think about work, our dogs also need some free time where they can enjoy romping and playing with the family or exploring the local woodland paths, rolling in the grass or lazing in the warm sunshine, and just being a dog.***

Depending on their age, the Staffordshire will usually be an energetic dog. He or she will generally have a lively and playful temperament that loves to chase and romp, and will be most happy and contented when given a job to do. Depending on what you're into, this Terrier may be a great hunting companion or a blue-ribbon performer in many different canine sports.

Supervision during play with other dogs is always important with this strong-willed and often imposing Terrier and in order to prevent possible squabbles, you will need to ensure that you are fully in control and capable of intervening to quickly shut down any unwanted situation should your puppy or young dog try to be dominant or overly bossy with other dogs.

While every dog is different, with respect to how much exercise they might need, how active YOU are will also have a definite effect. You can learn much more about the exercises that will keep this dog happy in Chapter 6 (Every Happy Staffordshire Bull Terrier Wants Exercise).

Happy Vet Visits

Even though you may be offering your dog the best food, being vigilant with exercising, socialising and carefully training your dog to be a calm and obedient member of your family, you will also want to schedule yearly visits to your chosen veterinarian's office to make sure all is well.

Begin taking your dog to the vet's office even when they don't have any reason to be there, other than to receive a friendly greeting and perhaps a treat from staff, so that your dog can get used to the different smells and people who work there because when you do this, your dog will learn that visits to the vet's office can be a happy experience.

While it's ideal to get your puppy used to visits to the vet's office when they are still young, there is much you can do throughout the life of your adult dog that will help to keep these visits to a minimum. Be sure to read Chapter 8 (Care of the Happy Staffordshire Bull Terrier) that outlines many things you can do to help ensure your dog remains as healthy as possible.

Back to the pen and paper exercise.

When you are attentive and observant, and take the time to think about the many things you can do that will keep your dog happy, even more ideas will present themselves along the way, and you and your chosen canine companion will enjoy a long and happy life together. Take my word for it, and *do make the time for this fun exercise* because you will thank me later.

In a Nutshell

The above paragraphs are a short synopsis of what I think makes for a Happy Staffordshire, and I'm sure you may have many more ideas to contribute to this list.

The following Chapters of this book contain much more detail concerning what every conscientious guardian needs to commit to, on a daily basis, in order to ensure that the human family and their chosen canine companion have the best possible opportunity for living a safe, happy and healthy life together.

When you want to raise a Happy canine companion that is a joy to share your life with, you will want to carefully read through the entire coming Chapters, while always keeping in mind, not just what makes you and your family happy, but what makes your dog happy as well.

Chapter 3: Overview of the Happy Staffordshire Bull Terrier

"If I could be half the person my dog is,
I'd be twice the human I am."
— Charles Yu

I cannot stress enough how important it is that you understand the basics of any breed you may be considering sharing your life with, such as size, energy level, intelligence, temperament, and exercise requirements. Once you are familiar with the basics, you can truly understand if you are the right person or family for sharing your life with a particular breed of dog.

When considering sharing your life with this strong and determined Terrier, there are several important points to keep in mind, including:

- this breed may be banned in many areas
- people may be afraid of this breed
- you may be denied insurance
- they can be aggressive toward unknown dogs
- they may have a strong prey drive
- confrontational energy from another dog may cause a fight

- you never want this dog to be the boss
- this dog needs a strong, confident human leader

Taking the time to learn about temperament, health and what function a breed was originally bred to perform will help you choose wisely when considering if your lifestyle and daily routine can meet this dog's needs.

History

It is believed that this strong, powerful and agile Terrier was first bred in the West Midlands of England. Even though they are also referred to as the *"American"* Staffordshire, they were named after the English county of Staffordshire where they were further developed.

During the earliest crossings of the Bulldog and Terrier, and before the name of Staffordshire Bull Terrier (or American Staffordshire Terrier) was agreed upon, the breed was also referred to by several different names, including *"Bull-and-Terrier Dog"*, *"Half and Half"* and *"Pit Bull"*.

These dogs were most likely developed in the first place by crossing the Bulldog with tenacious Terriers, because of the perceived need for smaller, more agile, vermin catchers and improved performers in the blood sport fighting ring - hence the name *"Pit Bull"*.

Early pictures of late 1800's Old English Bulldogs (now extinct) closely resemble the Staffordshire Bull Terrier, which is quite likely why it is believed that the ancestors of this breed include crossings of the early Bulldog with the Black and Tan (now called the Manchester) Terrier, Fox Terrier and White English Terrier.

DID YOU KNOW? ***This dog has been through many name changes, creating much confusion between the "English Staffordshire Bull Terrier", the "Staffordshire Terrier", the "American Pit Bull Terrier" and the "American Staffordshire Terrier", and while***

there are differences, depending on whom you talk to, they are often considered the same dog.

The name "American Staffordshire" Terrier was adopted in 1972, apparently in an attempt to distinguish between the more refined build of the Staffordshire Bull Terrier of England with the slightly heavier version developed in the United States.

When these dogs began to find their way into the United States, during the late 1800's, they were first referred to as "Pit Dogs" and "Pit Bull Terriers", then "American Bull Terriers" or "Yankee Terriers" and now they are also known as the "Amstaff" and nicknamed "Staffy" or "Staffords".

As an adorable puppy, this Terrier needs to quickly learn their place in the family and what they can or cannot get away with before they become too stubborn, strong or headstrong to handle.

This is an athletic, powerful dog that while requiring rigorous daily exercising to maintain their muscle tone, craves human attention and companionship and wants to always be at your side.

While usually calm by nature and peaceful with other pets they have grown up with, they are high spirited and strong-willed and he or she will need to be closely supervised around unknown dogs, because they will be more than willing to fight should they feel challenged.

Be aware that even though this dog is very loyal and affectionate with their family, you should never scrimp on socialising, vigorous exercising and teaching consistently firm rules and boundaries and always be on guard when out and about in areas where unknown animals or dogs may cross your path.

Many people mistake the Staffordshire Bull Terrier for a Pit Bull, and although they are similar, and in the past were also fearless pit brawlers, today responsible breeders are vigilant about producing sweet-natured family dogs that are patient, gentle and affectionate with children.

Despite careful breeding practises and standards, these dogs often retain the tenacious fighting instinct around unknown dogs, which means early and on-going socialisation is a MUST, so that he or she will be sure to learn good manners.

Recognized by the American Kennel Club (AKC) in 1936, this sturdy, muscular and imposing canine is a rugged, impulsive, people-oriented companion with a confident temperament that currently holds the #82 popularity position amongst the 193 AKC registered purebreds.

Many well-known actors, including Kevin Bacon, Jessica Alba, Liam Hemsworth and Linda Blair have shared their lives with the Staffordshire Bull Terrier.

OK, now that you have a basic understanding of the history of this loyal and chunky canine, following is the main overview of the breed, which will be the foundation of wisely choosing and raising a happy and well-behaved dog.

Staffordshire Bull Terrier Vital Statistics

While every dog is unique, there are standards that are common to each purebred canine, such as height, weight and various coat types, colours and features. You can also get a pretty good idea of what the puppies will look like when full grown, when you see their parents.

Height and Weight

When measured at the shoulder on average, this sturdy, medium-sized, muscular dog may stand between 14 and 16 inches (35 and 41 centimetres) and ideally weigh between 24 and 38 pounds (11 and 17 kilograms) or more or less, depending on the size of both breed parents, with an average lifespan of between 12 and 14 years.

Coat Colors and Common Features

This solid Terrier has a deep chest, sturdy, very muscular and almost square body, with a short, broad muzzle, wide mouth, strong jaws, and a smooth, close fitting coat.

The eyes are round-shaped and usually dark in colour. The rose shaped or half-pricked ears are medium size with rounded tips, and the nose colour will be black.

This dog's medium length, straight, low set tail is not docked and will be strong at the root, tapering to a point at the end. Acceptable coat colours include black, blue, brindle, fawn, red, white, and may be with or without white markings.

The single coat of the Staffy will be short and shiny, with a stiff feel to the touch and will shed all year round, requiring regular brushing every few days to remove dead hair and keep them looking their best.

DID YOU KNOW? ***In England, despite their tough look, this Terrier is nicknamed the "nanny dog" because of its reputation as a vigilant guardian and gentle child's playmate.***

How Smart is the Staffordshire Bull Terrier?

While every dog is surprisingly different even within the same breed, despite what some "experts" might have to say about it, you need to keep in mind that there are *"people smarts"* and *"dog smarts"* and that these two ways of rating intelligence are often widely divergent or in conflict with one another.

If you really want to rate your dog's intelligence, based on what we humans think is *"smart"*, there is a book *("The Intelligence of Dogs")* written in 1994 by Stanley Coren, which has become the standard for rating the particular intelligence of different canine breeds.

While I can agree, in part, with some of the information contained in this book, I can also disagree. I have much personal experience with many breeds, and while I concur with the moderately high smarts rating for the Staffordshire, I have found that some dogs that are rated very low on the intelligence scale are also very smart in their own way.

Therefore, I caution you not to pre-handicap your dog's level of intelligence just because of something you may have read in a well-respected book, because each dog has their own unique set of talents and much of how they develop mentally is up to their guardian.

Coren judges canine intelligence of particular purebred canines based on three categories, as follows:

*"**Instinctive Intelligence** – a dog's ability to carry out tasks it was bred to perform, such as guarding, herding, hunting, pointing, retrieving or supplying companionship."*

*"**Adaptive Intelligence** – how well a dog is able to solve problems on its own."*

*"**Working/Obedience Intelligence** – how quickly a dog is able to learn from humans."*

The Staffordshire Bull Terrier is a very smart dog that will usually be eager to learn and easy to train so long as you demonstrate to him or her that you have strong enough energy to lead them. Coren places this strong-willed dog in the #48 position out of 138 listed breeds in the *"Above Average Working Dogs"* category.

Please keep in mind that there are always exceptions to every study and a particular breed's degree of intelligence is often related to their early upbringing and how they are trained.

I have had personal experience with this breed, and can tell you that they are indeed eager to please and quick to learn. When you are firm with them and use fair and positive training methods that involve treat rewards, this will be an intelligent, versatile and willing to learn dog that will be highly trainable.

When training a puppy, be patient, consistent and no more than 5 to 10 minutes each time. It's important to learn when enough is enough so your puppy doesn't become overwhelmed and simply zone out.

DID YOU KNOW? ***Many other dog breeds have difficulty "reading" the Staffy's body language because of their very wide mouth, which they can misinterpret as an aggressive stance.***

If this dog is misbehaving, it's most likely because they are bored and frustrated, and they need much more exercise. This energetic dog needs something to do that stretches their mind and body, and if you don't provide them with consistent, daily, sufficient mental and physical exercise, this dog will become stressed and unhappy.

Make sure that your training involves fair, firm guidance and discipline and plenty of socialising from a young age, so that he or she will listen to your commands, respect the rules and boundaries you've taught, and trust and follow you as their leader.

FACT ***Any humans that don't have the confidence and sufficient knowledge to properly socialise, train, establish and then consistently enforce rules, may soon find themselves in trouble if they let this strong-willed, muscular and very powerful dog take the lead.***

Staffordshire Bull Terriers are sturdy, agile and energetic athletes with great stamina that can excel in any sort of advanced training or obedience competition, where retrieving and jumping skills are required, or in Agility (obstacle course) competitions, where speed is required.

Temperament of the Staffordshire Bull Terrier

The versatile Staffordshire Bull is a medium-sized dog with a very self-assured attitude that usually has a calm temperament and is often described as stubborn, active, friendly, affectionate, loyal, and fun-loving.

He or she may have a high prey drive, which means they could love to chase small, fast-moving prey, such as birds, squirrels, rabbits, vermin, or the neighbour's cat.

Be aware that this Terrier usually has a strong mind of his or her own and can easily become obsessed with the ball retrieving game. Make sure you don't inadvertently create a "ball crazed" dog by teaching them early on that it is you who are the boss, not the ball. This type of training will involve your fur friend learning patience that may seriously try your own.

This vigilant, playful Terrier loves and needs a lot of physical exercise every day, and if you allow them to lounge about the house all day, they will quickly gain weight.

All this dog really wants to do is play, run around and spend time with the humans they love. They will be happy so long as they are involved in whatever activity is up for grabs, whether it's walking, hiking, biking, running, swimming, reading a book or taking a nap with their people.

Most Staffordshire Bull Terriers are sturdy, energetic, alert and faithful companions always eager for the next adventure and may be a good choice for active families with older children who understand how to respect a dog's space. You will want to keep in mind that this dog tends toward becoming overly attached to their humans, which means that he or she can be a candidate for developing separation anxiety.

This dog could also be a great companion for older adults who know how to handle a stronger breed and have the energy, time and mobility required to provide the vigorous daily exercise and mental stimulation this fun-loving companion will need.

reminder ***This dog loves to play, so a living space that includes a back yard where they can burn off energy chasing a ball or retrieving will be ideal.***

Unfortunately, sometimes people choose the Staffordshire Bull Terrier as a companion based on all the wrong reasons, including:

- those pleading puppy eyes
- their medium size
- feeling sorry for a dog surrendered to a rescue or the SPCA
- fond childhood memories of a neighbour's dog
- their sturdy build and fearless nature
- their tough dog reputation
- their best friend has the same breed
- their playful and loyal temperament
- their star status from being featured in movies and on TV

To choose any dog as your companion based on these superficial criteria could end up being a BIG mistake that you will soon regret. Rather, you need to consider the energetic and playful temperament of this breed and their strong desire for plenty of attention and daily exercise while not forgetting that, warranted or not, many people may be afraid of this dog.

When this dog is chosen for the wrong reasons, once the puppy cute factor has worn off, and the family becomes distracted with other areas of their life, the result could inevitably be an unhappy, frustrated and under-exercised dog that suffers from boredom and may soon become destructive and/or unhealthily overweight.

Any dog that is routinely unchallenged by moderate to high daily activity and mental stimulation, especially an intelligent and active one that comes from a working background, may develop problematic behaviours.

Unwanted behaviours with a bored Staffordshire can be many, and as an example may include:

- eating baseboards
- raiding the garbage
- chewing holes in walls
- destroying furniture
- excessive barking
- killing the neighbour's cat
- fighting with unknown dogs
- destructive hole digging in your back yard
- escaping the house or yard entirely

TIP ***If you make the mistake of thinking your dog will be safe left all alone in your fenced back yard, and still be there when you return home, think again. You may be surprised at how determined this athletic companion is and what they will do to escape boredom in search of something interesting to chase.***

The Staffordshire lives for play and adventure and if left alone for long hours they will be very unhappy, which could encourage them to become a talented escape artist. The agile and intelligent Staffy may figure out how to escape from confinement by using their strong legs to jump fences, climb fences, dig under fences or find cracks they can squeeze through if they want to get out. When this dog is bored and lonely, they usually WILL want to get out because they always want to be with their human family or engaged in some sort of interesting task or routine that challenges both body and mind.

When you have a compatible, active lifestyle and are able to keep this smart dog at your side throughout the majority of your days, and teach with a firm, yet kind and consistent approach, he or she will be a highly trainable companion you will be proud to call your best friend.

Every dog needs the discipline of being regularly walked on leash outside of the home each day, as well as the opportunity for off-leash time to run and play fetch or enjoy socialising with other dogs under your close supervision.

The temperament of a Staffy will vary from dog to dog, and be somewhat dependent upon breeding lines and their first weeks with the breeder, as well as the human guardian who has trained and socialised them during the first few months of their life. Generally speaking, however, under the rough and tough looking exterior lurks a sweet, playful, agile, energetic and loving breed that wants to always be in close contact with their human guardians.

Proper socialising and teaching basic commands should begin at a young age for the smart Staffordshire, who can begin to learn basic commands at eight to ten weeks of age.

When treated fairly and trained with firm, positive reinforcement, this Terrier will have a zest for learning new things very quickly and will love the attention any sort of training program provides.

TIP ***This is a strong and fearless Terrier that will not hesitate to fight back if they feel they are being challenged. Therefore, without sufficient socialisation, a guardian should always be***

watchful when their dog is in the presence of unfamiliar dogs, people, animals or circumstances.

Generally speaking, the personality of the Staffordshire Bull Terrier and how they develop will depend on whether they are bred from a social or antisocial line, and the skill of their human guardian when raising them.

BOTTOM LINE: this lively Terrier will be happy so long as you engage them in moderate daily walks, high energy running free time, a vigorous canine sport, or perhaps spend time teaching him or her various tricks and routines.

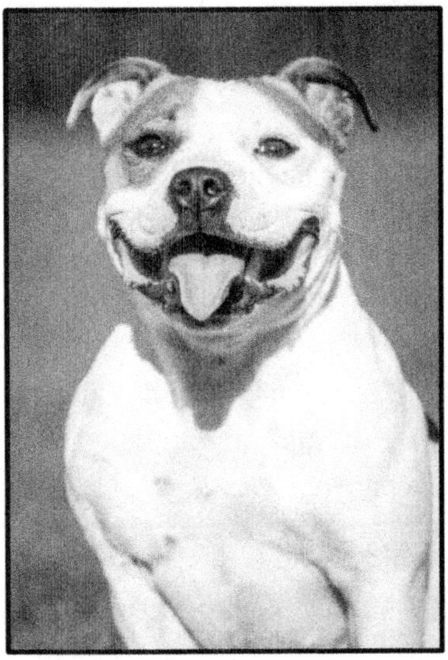

The muscular and tenacious adult Staffordshire is certainly capable of excelling at several canine sports, such as Agility, Flyball, Disc Dog, or perhaps even learning how to skateboard.

Whatever you teach this dog, at a minimum, make sure that you always get them outside for several daily, 30-60 minute walks and allow them some off-leash time to freely run, swim, fetch and sniff and learn proper socialising skills with other dogs.

The highest priority for a Staffy is always that they are kept busy with play, vigorous daily exercise, and being included in family outings and activities because this also helps to socialise and prevent them from becoming bored.

When they are puppies, it's important to engage them in thinking and working activities because they need this stimulation as part of their on-going healthy development.

As you can well imagine, how active you are will have a sizeable impact on the health of your Terrier. Remember that without sufficient daily activity this dog may soon become lethargic, overweight and unhealthy.

All puppies are energetic, including this puppy, and if you are active with them at a young age, and engage them in training and activities that stretch their minds and bodies, chances are that they will continue to be active well into their senior years.

On the other hand, if you tend toward being more of a couch potato human, the chances are high that this dog will become lazy, overweight, bored and very unhappy, which can lead to unwanted behaviours and exacerbated health problems.

While this fearless Terrier can be just as happy living in a rural setting, or enjoying the city lifestyle, keep in mind that he or she may retain a strong prey drive, and if you do not find safe ways to consistently address their natural abilities, they may display their feelings through destructive chewing, digging or excessive barking.

Staffordshire Bull Terrier Special Needs

This powerful, muscular Terrier is super affectionate with their family and needs plenty of close human contact and playful loving interaction with their humans throughout the day.

Often strong-willed and stubborn, this dog needs to be extensively socialised and properly trained, because without strong direction from their human to teach them what is OK and what is not, they have the potential for becoming aggressive, especially if they are forced into making human decisions when faced with unfamiliar situations.

DID YOU KNOW? ***There is a story about a famous Staffordshire Bull Terrier named "Stubby" that was the most decorated war dog of the First World War (read more below).***

Sergeant Stubby: Born 1916 or 1917 - Died March 16, 1926

This brindle-coated Staffy rose from stray wandering an army training field in Connecticut to bravely serving in the trenches with the 102nd French Infantry for 18 months during World War I. Stubby was the only dog to be promoted through combat to the rank of sergeant after participating in four offensives and 17 battles and being injured by shrapnel and gas attacks.

Stubby became sensitive to the smell of gas and learned to warn his unit of poison gas attacks and letting his unit know when to run for cover. He was also a mercy dog that would search the field for injured soldiers and stay with them until paramedics arrived.

Stubby was honoured by the Red Cross, the American Legion, and the YMCA, and also awarded a gold medal by the Humane Education Society for service to his country.

In order to keep the curious and active Staffordshire happy, they really need ***to be engaged in*** a wide variety of interesting tasks to keep them busy. Consider teaching this dog tricks, routines and canine sports that will challenge their doggy smarts and appeal to their strong work ethic.

This feisty Terrier needs early and on-going socialisation and training so that they don't take over or become possessive of their humans and/or aggressive with other dogs and animals.

Consider training this dog to jog with you on a "Springer Bicycle Jogger" (**pictured**) that attaches to your bicycle, so they can receive a good amount of disciplined exercise in a short period of time, while still safely under your control.

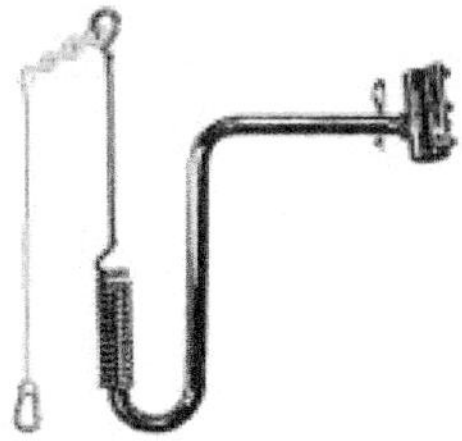

Keep in mind that making sure this energetic dog is happy and contented may involve more time and attention than a first-time dog guardian or otherwise occupied family is able to provide.

Keep in mind that while conscientious breeders now breed for different characteristics than what was desirable in this dog's ancestors, this Terrier may still retain more or less of their original vermin chasing and pit fighting urges. This means that he or she may display a strong desire to chase small creatures and they will most likely firmly stand their ground against any dog that displays a challenging front. Depending on how strong this dog's hunting instinct may be, and how well trained they are, you may need to keep this fearless companion on leash when out walking in areas where they could get into trouble.

Happy Staffordshire Bull Terrier Secrets

The Staffordshire Bull Terrier was named after the English county of Staffordshire, where they originated in the city of Birmingham in the West Midlands.

This dog's courageous ancestors were primarily bred for the now illegal blood sport of rat baiting and dog fighting.

The Staffordshire Bull Terrier has become a popular companion breed in their home country as well as in Australia, France, and New Zealand.

DID YOU KNOW? ***In 2019, based on a poll of 10,000 people, the Staffordshire Bull Terrier was named Britain's favourite dog breed.***

Famous conservationist, TV show host of the "Crocodile Hunter", Steve Irwin raised his Stafford named "Sui" from a puppy. She had a great life because she was always part of his adventures, whether wrangling wild pigs, snakes, crocodiles or babysitting Irwin's daughter.

This bright and active dog likes to have a job to do, and if you have the time and patience, there is no end to what you could teach the loyal Staffy.

FACT ***As a result of this dog being bred to exterminate vermin, they may retain a very strong attraction to fast moving objects, such as balls and Frisbees, which makes them a tireless participant for playing fetch or Flyball.***

Despite the bad press this dog has received over the years, with the right guardian, the Staffy can be an affectionate, fun-loving, playful, well behaved and loyal family companion that could be the perfect dog for you.

In a Nutshell

Familiarizing yourself with the Staffordshire Bull Terrier breed, their early history and special needs, plus understanding their intelligence level, determined temperament and high exercise requirements will help you to decide if this robust dog, that has a vast following of fans, is the right companion for you and your family.

Taking the time to understand the breed's needs will not only save you and your dog from much future grief, but it will be a pre-requisite for raising a content, well-behaved, and happy dog that you are proud to call your best friend and companion.

Chapter 4: Healthy Staffordshire Bull Terrier = Happy Dog

"Dogs are not our whole life,
but they make our lives whole."
— Roger Caras

If your Staffordshire Bull Terrier is not physically healthy, he or she will not be a happy canine companion for very long, because suffering from health-related issues can easily create a miserable and ill-mannered dog.

There are many steps you can take that will help to ensure that you are doing all that you can to keep on top of your Staffy's best health.

Make sure you choose a veterinarian that can provide yearly check-ups, spay or neuter in a timely fashion, research a healthy diet for him or her, and take the time to read through this section so that you are aware of issues that could adversely affect your dog's health.

As well, take the time to learn a little canine CPR, because doing so may save the life of your dog, or even someone else's.

Below you will find more information that may help you raise a healthy and happy dog.

Choose Your Veterinarian Wisely

Some clinics specialize in caring for smaller pets, while some specialize in larger animal care, and others have a wide-ranging area of expertise and will care for all animals, including livestock and reptiles.

Choosing an appropriate veterinary clinic will be very similar to choosing the right doctor or health care clinic for your own personal health. You want to ensure that your dog receives the quality care they deserve, so take some time to find a suitable vet. A good place to begin your search will be by asking other dog owners where they take their furry friends and whether they are happy with the service they receive.

TIP ***Take your Staffy into your chosen clinic several times before they actually need to be there for any treatment, so that they are not fearful of the new smells and unfamiliar surroundings.***

Consider Timely Neutering or Spaying

While opinions vary regarding the best time to neuter or spay a young dog, one thing that many do agree upon is that earlier spaying or neutering, between the ages of 4 and 6 months, can be a preferable choice than waiting longer.

Non-neutered or spayed males and females are more likely to display aggression related to sexual behaviour, than are dogs that have been neutered or spayed.

As well, fighting, particularly between male dogs, is less common after neutering. Also, the intensity of other types of aggression, such as irritable aggression in females will usually be totally eliminated after spaying, so make that appointment at the vet's office and get it done.

Effects on General Temperament: often we humans become needlessly worried that a neutered or spayed dog will lose their vigour, when in fact, you will be acting as an informed, caring and conscientious guardian by helping to diminish or eliminate many undesirable qualities that can be the result of hormonal impact.

Effects on Escape and Roaming: a neutered or spayed dog is less likely to wander, and castrated male dogs have the tendency to patrol smaller sized outdoor areas and are less likely to participate in territorial rivalry with other dogs they may perceive as challengers.

Possible Weight Gain: while metabolic changes that occur after spaying or neutering can cause some puppies to gain weight, often the real culprit for any weight gain is the human feeling guilty for subjecting their puppy to this medical procedure, and in an attempt to make themselves feel better, they feed more treats or meals to their companion.

TIP ***If you notice weight gain after neutering or spaying your puppy, simply adjust their food and treat consumption as needed and once stitches are healed, make sure that they are receiving adequate daily exercise.***

Educate Yourself About Vaccinations

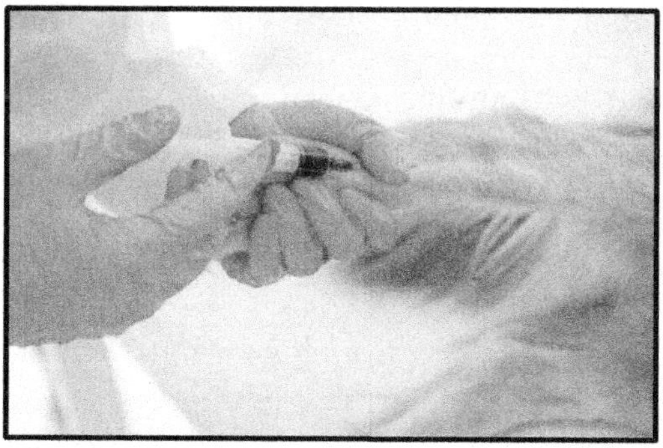

Currently it has become common practice to vaccinate adult dogs every three years. If your veterinarian is adamant about a yearly vaccination for your puppy, ask them why, because to do otherwise is considered by many professionals to be *"over vaccinating"*.

Be proactive and ask your vet to give your dog a blood test because this is a simple way to determine whether or not he or she actually needs a booster.

Puppies need to be vaccinated in order to provide them with protection against four common and serious diseases referred to as ***"DAPP"***, which stands for Distemper, Adenovirus, Parainfluenza and Parvo Virus.

Approximately one week after your puppy has completed all three sets of primary DAPP vaccinations, they will be fully protected from those specific diseases.

Be Aware of the Health Conditions That May Affect Your Dog

A healthy, happy Staffordshire Bull Terrier may live to be 12 to 15 years (on average), and with sufficient mental and physical exercise, proper care and an appropriately nutritious diet they may not suffer from any of the below noted health concerns.

However, it is still prudent to list all concerns possibly associated with the Staffordshire breed so that you have a clear understanding of problems that *"may"* affect your dog, including:

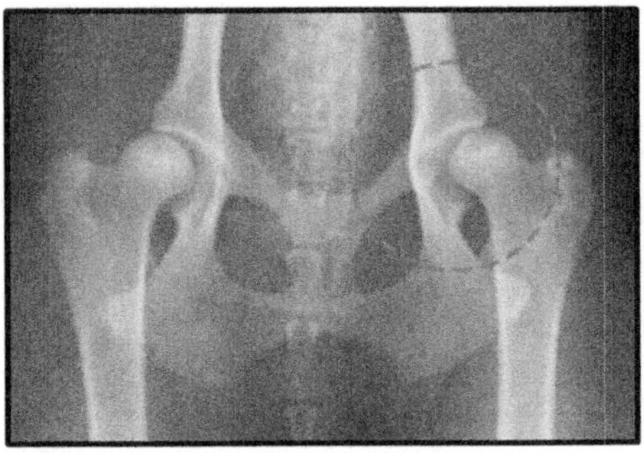

Hip Dysplasia (pictured): is a degenerative disease in which the hip joint becomes weakened due to abnormal growth. Depending upon the severity of the disease, treatment will involve medication or surgery. Screening of the parents cannot guarantee that puppies will not be born with this problem.

This is a musculoskeletal issue commonly seen in the Staffy breed. Hip dysplasia occurs when the head of the femur or thigh bone slips out of its rightful place in the hip socket. When the bone is out of joint, it can cause the dog to limp or it might cause total limb lameness. Over time, the wear and tear on the joints can lead to painful inflammation, which may necessitate a surgical repair. In more mild cases, other treatment options include pain medications and anti-inflammatories.

Osteochondritis: is a joint disorder that causes cracks to form in the cartilage and underlying bone and is caused by lack of blood flow to the cartilage, which then results in the bone dying and being absorbed by the dog's body. When this occurs, the joint can no longer move freely and movement causes discomfort, pain and more damage.

Causes can be due to trauma, poor nutrition, genetics or improper or too strenuous exercising at an early age and can affect the shoulder, knee, elbow or hock joints. Diagnosis requires x-ray and restricted activity. In severe cases, surgery will be required to remove the defective cartilage.

Obesity: the Staffordshire Bull Terrier is already a sturdy and stout dog and without adequate exercise and too much food may easily become obese, which can lead to joint problems and heart disease.

Cataracts (see picture): like many dogs, the Staffordshire Bull Terrier can suffer from cataracts that cause the lens of the eye to become opaque or cloudy, leading to blindness.

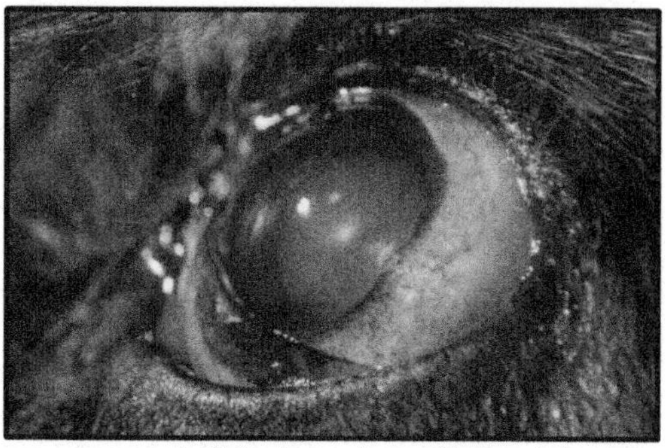

While this disease usually occurs in old age, it can also appear in a younger dog and treatment involves surgical removal.

Technically speaking, a cataract is an opacity that forms in the lens of the eye and it can partially or completely obstruct your dog's vision. Though cataracts are not painful, there is a slight risk that the cataract could slip out of place and float around the eye or it could become stuck in the tear duct, blocking fluid drainage.

Unfortunately, cataracts cannot be prevented, especially if it is a condition your puppy inherited genetically. If the cataract is caught while still in the early stages, however, your vet may be able to take steps to slow the progression and maybe even save your dog's vision. In some cases, a dog's vision can be restored by surgically removing the cataract, however, there is a fairly long recovery period for this kind of surgery.

Progressive Retinal Atrophy (PRA): causes degeneration of the retina, which is part of the eye. The retina is the part that senses visual information and sends it to the brain. Degeneration of this vital part of the eye eventually will lead to blindness. This disease usually appears between 3 and 5 years of age. A simple DNA test is available to determine without waiting for symptoms to appear.

Entropion: is a condition in which the dog's eyelid will roll inward which then causes the lashes to rub against the eyeball. Left untreated, this condition can severely damage the dog's eye, even causing blindness. Surgery is required to correct this problem.

Congenital Deafness: inherited deafness affects quite a number of dog breeds and in most cases is associated with white coat coloration around the head, as this is linked to the piebald and/or merle genes. Deafness usually occurs in puppies within a few weeks of birth and it can occur in only one ear, or both ears.

There is no cure and puppies that are deaf in both ears are often euthanized because they are accident prone, startle easily, which can lead to biting, and they can be difficult to train.

Hypothyroidism: 20% of this breed suffer from this condition, which results from an inadequate production of thyroid hormone and is treated with medication. Symptoms can include weight gain or obesity, constant hunger, reduced energy and a coarser feel to the dog's coat texture. Blood samples will be taken in order to test for a malfunctioning thyroid.

Subaortic Stenosis: is a congenital narrowing in the area of the pulmonary heart valve located between the pulmonary artery and the right ventricular chamber of the dog's heart. Narrowing in this area impairs normal blood flow through the artery. When this happens, blood flow can be seriously interrupted which then leads to right-sided heart failure. This condition may be first diagnosed when hearing a heart murmur under stethoscopic examination. Dogs displaying clinical signs of heart failure are treated with diuretics.

Cardiomyopathy: is a disease of the heart that causes weakness in the muscle tissues and a subsequent enlarging of the heart, which can lead to heart failure.

Bloat (Emergency Gastrointestinal Syndrome): is a life-threatening, common occurrence that can affect any size of deep-chested canine. This condition can happen quickly, especially if you feed your dog right after vigorous exercise, or if they are a very fast eater and gulp in large quantities of air with their food.

The stomach then distends with gas and fluid which can cause the stomach to twist 180-degrees or more. When the stomach is closed off, the food is then trapped inside where it will ferment and cause the stomach to bulge. The bulging stomach can then interfere with blood circulation and obstruct veins in the abdomen, causing low blood pressure, followed by shock and damage to internal organs.

Bloat is a serious, life-threatening condition (50% of dogs that develop bloat do not survive) that requires immediate veterinary intervention. If you have a deep chested dog that tends to gulp their food, get them a slow feeder type of bowl to slow down their eating process and never feed them immediately after exercise or having had a large drink of water.

Pyoderma: is a bacterial infection of the dog's skin that causes itching and redness that can lead to lesions on the skin that are similar to pimples. Treatment involves shampoo and antibiotic creams.

Demodectic Mange: is a skin disease known by several names, including "red mange", "follicular mange" or "puppy mange", caused by the Demodex canis mite, and usually in young dogs or puppies. This disease is caused by a weak, poorly developed or suppressed immune system that is unable to keep the spread of these mites, which are passed from mother to puppy under control.

Most puppies are immune to the effect of these microscopic mites and the few that are not develop hair loss, or red, crusty lesions, usually around the head. Most will heal without intervention as the puppy matures and the dog's immune system grows stronger. In persistent cases, treatment involves the application of topical medication.

Mast Cell Tumors: are a form of cancer tumors originating from bone marrow and found within the connective tissues throughout the dog's body.

When you take good care of your happy Staffordshire Bull Terrier 's health, and they come from a trusted breeder, he or she may never have to suffer from any of the above-noted list of health problems.

FACT ***If your Staffy is an avid participant in the ball retrieving game, DO NOT use tennis balls because they are made with fiberglass that will wear down your dog's teeth. Instead, choose only balls that are certified safe for dogs.***

Educate Yourself About Common Canine Diseases and Viruses

While your dog may never suffer from a common disease or virus, in order to ensure the safety and health of your happy Staffordshire, it's a good idea to be aware of the many common diseases and viruses that could detrimentally affect the health of your dog.

Always watch out for the symptoms of the following common diseases and if you suspect that your dog has been infected, contact your vet immediately.

Distemper (sometimes called *"hard pad disease"*): is a contagious, serious, and deadly viral illness that is spread through the air or by direct or indirect contact with a dog (or other animal) that is already infected (such as ferrets, raccoons, foxes, skunks and wolves), that can also cause thickening of the pads on the feet or nose.

Early symptoms include fever, loss of appetite and mild eye inflammation that may only last a day or two, with symptoms becoming more serious and noticeable as the disease progresses. There is no known cure.

Adenovirus: causes infectious canine hepatitis, which can range in severity from very mild to very serious. The treatment focuses on management of symptoms, and the condition can sometimes result in death. Symptoms can vary and may include coughing, loss of appetite, increased thirst and urination, tiredness, vomiting and seizures.

Canine Parainfluenza Virus (CPIV): also referred to as *"canine influenza virus"*, *"greyhound disease"* or *"race flu"*, which is easily spread through the air or by coming into contact with respiratory secretions. While it is usually a self-limiting virus that will run its course within a couple of weeks, in severe cases and without antibiotic treatment, it may be fatal.

Symptoms can include a dry, hacking cough, difficulty breathing, wheezing, runny nose and eyes, sneezing, fever, loss of appetite, tiredness, depression and possible pneumonia. In cases where only a cough exists, tests will be required to determine whether the cause of the cough is the parainfluenza virus or the less serious *"kennel cough"*.

Canine Parvovirus (CPV): is a highly contagious viral illness affecting puppies and dogs, foxes, coyotes and wolves. Symptoms include vomiting, bloody diarrhoea, weight loss, and lack of appetite. Without prompt and proper treatment, dogs that have severe parvovirus infections can die within 48 to 72 hours.

Treatment will involve addressing dehydration and correcting electrolyte imbalances by administering intravenous fluids. Anti-inflammatory and antibiotic drugs are also given to control or prevent septicaemia, as well as drugs to control diarrhoea and vomiting.

Other Diseases and Viruses to Be Aware Of

What is Zoonotic? Zoonotic means a contagious disease that can be spread between both animals and humans.

Rabies: is a viral, zoonotic disease transmitted by coming into contact with the saliva of an infected animal, usually through a bite. The virus travels to the brain along the nerves and once symptoms develop (usually marked by a change in temperament), after a prolonged period of suffering, death is almost certainly inevitable. There is no treatment.

In most countries, vaccination against rabies is mandatory between the ages of twelve and sixteen weeks. If you plan to travel out of State or across country borders, you will need to make sure that your dog has an up-to-date Rabies Vaccination Certificate (NASPHV form 51) indicating they have been inoculated against rabies.

Leishmaniasis: is a contagious zoonotic infection caused by a parasite and is transmitted by a bite from a sand fly. While treatment involves the administration of a special drug (sodium stibogluconate), there is no definitive answer for effectively combating Leishmaniasis (especially since one vaccine will not prevent the known multiple species), with the prognosis often being fatal.

Symptoms may include loss of appetite, diarrhoea, severe weight loss, exercise intolerance, vomiting, nosebleed, tarry feces, fever, pain in the joints, excessive thirst and urination, inflammation of the muscles, and death from kidney failure.

Lyme Disease: this is one of the most common zoonotic tick-borne diseases in the world, which is transmitted by Borrelia bacteria found in the deer or sheep tick. Symptoms of this disease in a young or adult dog include recurrent lameness from joint inflammation, loss of appetite, depression, stiff walk with arched back, sensitivity to touch, swollen lymph nodes, fever, kidney damage, as well as rare heart or nervous system complications.

Control of the symptoms involves a lengthy course of antibiotic treatment in order to completely eliminate the organism.

Rocky Mountain Spotted Fever (RMSF): this is a zoonotic disease transmitted by both the American dog tick and the RMSF tick, which must be attached to the dog for a minimum of five hours in order to transmit the disease.

Common symptoms include fever, reduced appetite, depression, painful joints, lameness, vomiting and diarrhoea, and some dogs may develop heart abnormalities, pneumonia, kidney failure, liver damage, or even neurological signs, such as seizures or unsteady, wobbly or stumbling gait. Treatment involves a 2-3 week course of antibiotics (Doxycycline or Tetracycline).

Ehrlichiosis: a tick-borne disease transmitted by both the brown dog tick and the Lone Star Tick, with common symptoms including depression, reduced appetite, fever, stiff and painful joints and bruising. The signs of infection typically occur less than a month after a tick bite and last for approximately four weeks. There is no vaccine available. Treatment involves a long course of antibiotics.

Anaplasmosis: deer ticks **(pictured)** and Western blacklegged ticks are carriers of the bacteria that transmit canine Anaplasmosis. However, there is also another form of Anaplasmosis (caused by a different bacteria) that is carried by the brown dog tick.

Because the deer tick also carries other diseases, some animals may be at risk of developing more than one tick-borne disease at the same time. Signs are similar to Ehrlichiosis and include painful joints, diarrhoea, fever, and vomiting, as well as possible nervous system disorders. Treatment involves administering the antibiotic Doxycycline for a 30-day period.

Tick Paralysis (pictured): this zoonotic infection is caused when ticks attach themselves to the skin and secrete a neurotoxin that adversely compromises the nervous system. Affected dogs show signs of weakness and limpness approximately one week after being first bitten.

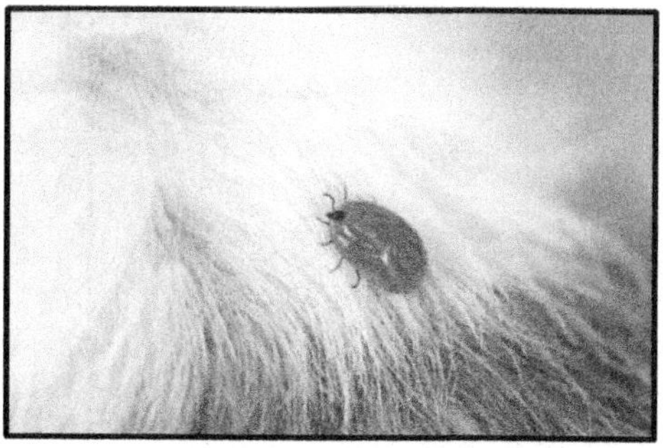

Symptoms usually begin with a change in pitch of the dog's usual bark, and weakness in the rear legs that eventually involves all four legs, followed by the dog having difficulty breathing and swallowing. Your dog can die if not diagnosed and properly treated by removal of the tick.

Canine Coronavirus: this highly contagious disease of the intestines, which is spread through the feces of contaminated dogs, while now a worldwide problem, can be destroyed by most commonly available disinfectants. Symptoms include diarrhoea, vomiting and weight loss or anorexia. There is a vaccine available, which is usually given to puppies, because they are more susceptible at a young age. Show dogs may also be vaccinated, because they have a higher risk of exposure to the disease.

Leptospirosis: is a worldwide zoonotic bacterial infection that can affect humans and many different kinds of animals, including dogs. There is potential for both humans and dogs to die from this disease if left untreated.

The good news is that this virus is usually treated with antibiotics and supportive care, and because you can protect your dog with a vaccination, it makes sense to vaccinate against this disease if you and your dog live in an area considered a hot spot for leptospirosis.

Be Aware: Allergies Can Adversely Affect Your Dog's Health

You may be surprised to learn that dogs may suffer from allergies in much the same way that people can. Not only can the Staffordshire Bull Terrier develop allergies to certain food ingredients, but he or she can also develop inhalant or contact allergies. The general signs of allergies include the following:

- Itchy red skin (**see picture below**)
- Itchy or runny eyes

- Licking the base of the tail
- Sneezing or coughing
- Ear infections
- Diarrhea
- Snoring from throat inflammation
- Chewing the paws

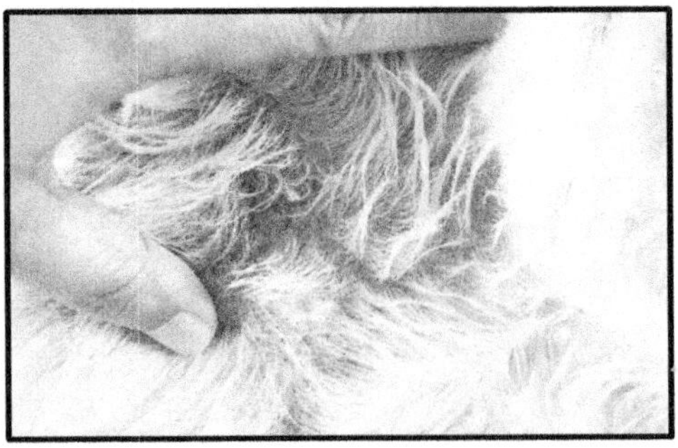

Some of the things that a dog can be allergic to include grass, weeds, pollen, mould spores, dust, dander, feathers, cigarette smoke, prescription drugs, perfumes, garden fertilizers and cleaning products. They can also be allergic to certain flea and tick products, so be very careful which one you choose. You should also never use products on your dog that are not designed specifically for dogs – this includes shampoo and conditioner.

One of the most common complaints discussed at the veterinarian's office when they see dogs obsessively scratching, biting, licking and chewing at their skin or paws is possible allergies, and there can be many triggers. When you educate yourself, you can help ensure your Terrier never has to suffer from allergies and can lead a healthier and happier life.

Environmental allergies: what many of us humans seem to forget is that our dogs can develop allergies to chemicals, car exhaust, dust, grass, mould, pollen, various forms of smoke, or flea and tick preparations, as well as allergies to materials such as cotton or wool, and chemicals found in washing soap or in cleaning products you use around your home.

Visual symptoms are usually first noticed on the dog's stomach, inside of their legs, and at their tail or paws. Because many allergies are seasonal, our dogs will often be more affected in the spring or fall, with some airborne irritants inhaled by your dog resulting in coughing, sneezing or watery eyes.

Pay attention and if you think that your dog may have come in contact with an irritant found somewhere in your environment, first give them a cleansing bath, with the proper canine shampoo and conditioner.

Junk food allergies: *"True"* food allergies usually account for only about 10% of allergy problems found in our canine friends.

Be aware that itching, chewing and chronic ear infections are not usually caused by food allergies, but rather are the result of a suppressed immune system, which may be the result of your dog consuming a low-quality diet. Food sensitivity issues can often be completely resolved by changing your dog's diet to a more easily digested, high-quality food.

For instance, check food ingredients on the label because far too many dog foods contain gluten products that are common allergens to our fur friends, such as corn, wheat and soybeans. Become a savvy label reader and ask questions, before you choose your dog's food.

<u>Take the Time to Learn a Little Canine CPR</u>

Of course, nobody wants to find his or herself in a situation where the life of their precious canine companion is put at risk. However, the reality is that accidents happen sometimes, and therefore knowing a little bit about how to help save your beloved furry friend (or maybe even someone else's) is valuable time well spent.

First of all, remember to handle an injured dog very carefully and gently. A dog that is traumatized, fearful or in pain, even one that is usually gentle, may lash out and try to bite.

Consider taking a class, because there are many animal CPR courses being offered these days through community educational systems or even online.

It's also a good idea to put together a canine first aid kit, both at home and in your vehicle, in case of emergencies, that includes the following items:

- Antiseptic Wash for wounds (hydrogen peroxide)
- Blanket
- Gauze Bandaging
- Kwik Stop styptic powder

- Medical Tape
- Nail Clippers
- Non-Stick Bandages for wounds
- Scissors
- Sterile Eye Wash
- Tick Twister
- Towel
- Tweezers
- Wash cloth

It would also be a smart idea to obtain a copy of the American Red Cross emergency techniques called *"Saving Your Pet With CPR"*, and familiarize yourself with the proper way to administer CPR to a dog.

Artificial Respiration Step by Step

If your dog becomes unconscious, depending upon what happened to them, they may stop breathing and if they stop breathing, they will go into cardiac arrest, when the heart stops beating and the dog dies.

However, after breathing stops, and before cardiac arrest, the heart can continue to beat for several minutes and this is when performing cardiopulmonary resuscitation (CPR) or artificial respiration can save your dog's life.

Step 1: place your dog on their side on a flat surface.

Step 2: check to make sure that your dog has actually stopped breathing by watching for the rise and fall of their chest and feel for their breath on your hand. Check the colour of your dog's gums, because lack of oxygen will make them turn blue.

Step 3: check that the dog's airway is clear and there is nothing stuck in their mouth or throat by extending the head and neck and opening your dog's mouth.

If there is an object blocking their throat, pull the tongue outward and use your fingers or pliers to get a firm grip on the object so that you can pull it free from the dog's throat. If you cannot reach the object that appears to be blocking the dog's airway passage, you will have to use the Heimlich Manoeuvre to try and dislodge it (see below).

Step 4: so long as the dog's airway is not blocked, you can lift their chin to straighten out the neck and begin rescue breathing.

Step 5: hold the dog's muzzle and close their mouth, put your mouth over the dog's nose and blow gently – just enough to cause the dog's chest to rise.

Step 6: wait long enough for the air you just breathed into the dog's lungs to leave before giving another breath.

Step 7: continue giving one gentle breath every 3 seconds as long as the heart is still beating and until your dog starts to breathe on their own.

Canine Heimlich Manoeuvre

If breath won't go in, the airway may be blocked. In this case, you will need to turn your dog upside down, with his or her back held against your chest.

Wrap your arms around the dog and clasp your hands together just below the dog's rib cage (since the dog is being held upside down, this will be actually above the rib cage, in the abdomen).

Using both arms, give five sharp thrusts to the abdomen, and then check the dog's mouth or airway for the object. If the object is visible, remove it, and give two more rescue breaths.

CPR Step by Step

If your dog's heart has stopped beating, then CPR must be started immediately and ideal would be to have one person performing the artificial respiration, while the other performs the CPR.

Step 1: put your dog on his or her side on a flat surface.

Step 2: feel for your dog's pulse or heartbeat by placing one hand over his or her left side, just behind the front leg.

Step 3: place the palm of your hand on your dog's rib cage over his or her heart, with your other hand on top of the first (for puppies, put just your thumb on one side of the chest and the rest of your fingers on the other side).

Step 4: press down and release, compressing the dog's chest approximately one inch (2-3 centimetres) and squeeze and release 80 to 100 times every minute.

While it's always the hope that you may never need to, if your dog is not breathing and there is no pulse, knowing what steps to take in an emergency (which includes how to do the doggy Heimlich Manoeuvre or apply compressions), could literally save the life of your own dog or maybe even someone else's.

In a Nutshell

While your dog may never have to suffer from any of the diseases or health problems that have been statistically known to affect the Staffordshire breed, you will probably still want to know what *may* afflict your dog because being aware of the signs can help him or her live a longer life.

As well, becoming familiar with emergency CPR procedures outlined in the following American Red Cross chart could help you save your dog's life.

It may also be prudent to take the time to choose a veterinarian that specializes in the care of small animals for yearly health check-ups, have your dog spayed or neutered in a timely fashion and educate yourself about required vaccinations.

Taking the steps outlined in this Chapter will help ensure that your dog will always have the best opportunity to be healthy and happy throughout your lifelong journey together.

Saving your pet with CPR

With pets increasingly being treated like a member of the family, many owners are learning emergency techniques like CPR to keep their pet alive before bringing it to a veterinarian.

If there is no breathing and no pulse, begin CPR immediately.

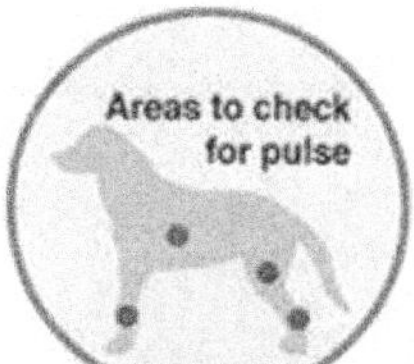

Check for breathing and pulse

Check pulse using middle and index finger below the wrist, inner thigh (femoral artery), below the ankle or where left elbow touches the chest.

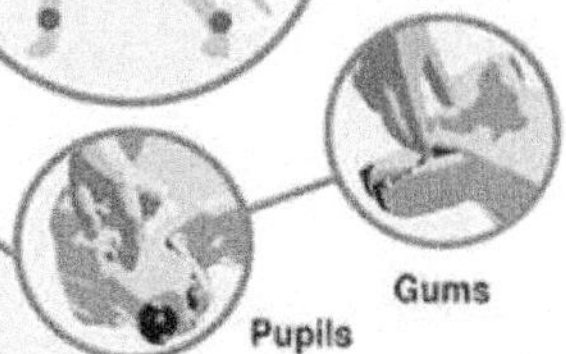

Look for other warning signs

- Gums and lips will appear gray- colored.
- Pupils will be dilated and not responsive to light.

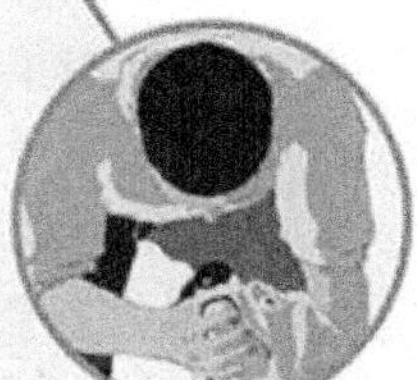

If not breathing, give breath to animal

Cats and small dogs

Place your mouth over its nose and mouth to blow air in.

Medium–large dogs

Place your mouth over its nose to blow air in.

Heimlich maneuver

If breath won't go in, airway may be blocked. Turn dog upside down, with its back against your chest. Wrap your arms around the dog and clasp your hands together just below its rib cage (since you're holding the dog upside down, it's above the rib cage, in the abdomen). Using both arms, give five sharp thrusts to the abdomen. Then check its mouth or airway for the object. If you see it, remove it and give two more rescue breaths.

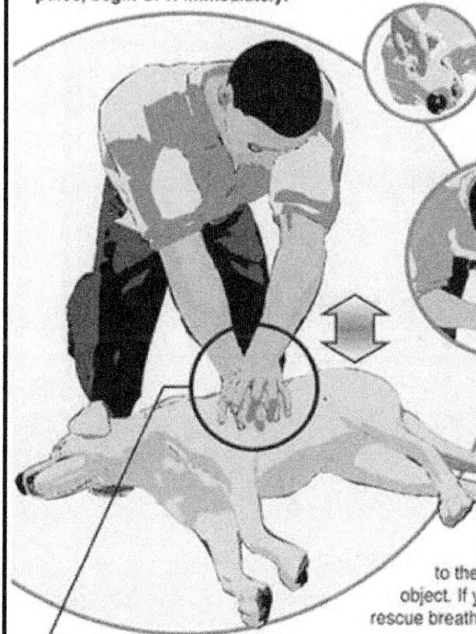

Start compressions if no pulse

Lay animal on right side and place hand over ribs where its elbow touches the chest. Begin compressions. Do not give compressions if dog has pulse.

Animal size	Compress chest	Compressions per breath of air
Cat/small dog (Under 30 lbs.)	1/2-1 inch	5
Medium–large dog (30–90 lbs.)	1–3 inches	5
Giant dog (over 90 lbs.)	1–3 inches	10

Repeat procedure

- Check pulse after 1 minute and then every few minutes.
- Continue giving CPR until the animal has a pulse and is breathing.
- Stop CPR after 20 minutes.

SOURCE: American Red Cross

Chapter 5: Let Your Dog BE a Happy Dog

"Don't make the mistake of treating your dogs like humans, or they'll treat you like dogs."
— Martha Scott

This chapter is written to alert you to the fact that because far too many of us humans have the tendency to treat our dogs more like human fur children than dogs, we can actually be the cause of future problems.

You need to understand that not allowing your fur friend to be *"dog-like"* is very important when we're talking about THEIR happiness, because treating a dog like a human can ultimately result in you creating any number of unwanted behavioural issues.

Your Dog is Not a Child

While this might sound like a strange thing to say, there is no doubt that many humans simply don't allow their dogs to actually BE dogs, because they are too busy confusing their dog and allowing them to be the boss by attributing human emotions to them, and treating them like children.

Today, the urge for humans to treat their dogs much more like children than dogs is becoming more and more of a serious problem, and perhaps contributing to this phenomenon is the fact that many Millennials are choosing to have dogs instead of children.

The reality is that no matter the size or breed of the dog, they still need to be accepted as dogs and they need their humans to lead them. When you begin to expect your dog to fulfill an emotional void that can only be met by another human, you may soon find yourself travelling down a road that can lead to many problems for both of you.

Yes, some dogs may need to wear clothing to provide protection from the cold and rain during the winter months. However, if the only reason you are dressing up your dog and treating them like a human child is because it makes you laugh, or appeals to a frustrated parental instinct, this may be a less than healthy relationship.

TIP ***With respect to canine clothing, if you live in a warm climate, you may want to provide your dog (especially one with a darker coat) with a cooling vest or a simple white t-shirt to reflect the heat during warmer summer months when they are walking outside in the sunshine.***

When your dog is a full-grown adult, you will definitely want to begin more complicated or advanced training sessions. They will enjoy the attention and time spent with you and when you have the desire and patience and they have the willingness, there is literally no end to what you can teach this energetic, loyal dog.

While some breeds of dogs of lower intelligence might be just fine without receiving daily interesting activities to keep them busy and mentally challenged, the Staffordshire Bull Terrier likes to work, and with their high intelligence and curious and playful temperament, they typically want and need to occupy much more of their guardian's time and energy by engaging in physical activities that also challenge them mentally.

A conscientious guardian of this breed will need to constantly be thinking of ways to challenge their bright and inquisitive canine companion to make this dog's daily life interesting.

If you and your dog are really enjoying learning new routines and tricks together, you might want to advance to teaching them the hand signals for *"commando crawl"*, how to *"speak"* or to *"jump through the human hoop"*, and depending on your particular dog, you may want to consider getting them involved in a fun canine sport, like Agility, Barn Hunt, Trick Training or even get them certified as a therapy dog.

TIP ***The only restriction to how far you can go with training your dog will be your imagination and their personal energy level, ability and desire to perform.***

Every one of our chosen canine companions has a uniquely wonderful set of gifts to share with their human counterparts, if only us humans would listen. They *"tell"* us when they are unhappy, frightened, bored, nervous, and when they are under-exercised, yet often we are not paying attention because we're caught up in our human world, or we just think they are being badly behaved.

If you are deciding to have dogs instead of children, be careful that you don't get caught up in attempting to manipulate your dog into being a furry child. Trying to turn a dog into a small, fur-covered human has had a seriously detrimental effect upon the health, happiness and behaviour of so many of our canine companions.

Single, lonely people often have dogs, which is just fine, so long as the human side of the equation doesn't expect their canine counterpart to fulfill what humans require on an emotional level, because this can be very confusing to a dog who needs their human to lead them.

FACT ***The Staffordshire Bull Terrier is not a breed well suited for the physically restricted or inactive or for humans that lead busy lives with long work schedules that keep them away from home. In order for this smart dog to be well balanced psychologically, they demand a lot of attention and will not be happy spending only a few minutes with their humans each day.***

This dog will also not be very happy leading a sedentary life because they have endless stamina and are highly energetic, curious and interested in what's going on around them. They need to get out and about on a regular basis, rather than simply lead the life of a couch potato.

In order to be the best guardians for our four-legged friends, and have a more harmonious relationship, we humans must have a better understanding of what our dogs need from us, rather than what we need from them. This way, our chosen canine companions can live in safety, harmony and security within our human environment.

Sadly, many of us humans are not well equipped to give our dogs what they really need, which is what leads to so many homeless, abandoned and frustrated dogs and so many overflowing rescue facilities.

As a professional dog whisperer who is regularly challenged with the task of finding amicable solutions for canine/human relationships that have become unbalanced, I can tell you with absolute certainty that once humans understand what needs to be changed and are willing to take the steps to do the work required, almost every stressful canine/human relationship can be turned into a happy one.

The sad part is that many humans are simply not aware of how important it is to really understand the breed they are choosing, or they don't factor in how much time they really have to do the consistent work and devote to ensuring that their chosen dog's needs are truly met.

Almost ALL canine problems, both mentally and physically, are a direct result of incompatible energy and lifestyle.

If you choose a dog without first seriously researching and being honest about your own lifestyle and how much time you truly can devote to a dog, you can almost be certain that problems will arise somewhere down the road.

It's no secret that lack of knowledge, acknowledging realistic time restraints or forgetting about taking a good look at our human lifestyle can be a typical human mistake when choosing the right dog. It's also no secret that if these important factors are not taken into consideration, learning about what their dog truly needs and being able to provide it will be a hit and miss undertaking that usually results in the "miss" coming out on top.

What we humans often forget to consider is that first and foremost, our dogs need to be respected for their unique canine qualities and we need to recognize and fully appreciate how willing they are to bend themselves to our will so that they can fit into our human environment.

For millennia, dog has been considered *"Man's best friend"*. In today's society, when we want to do the best for our canine companions and create a harmonious, mutually beneficial relationship, we humans need to spend more time receiving the proper training WE need, so that we can learn how to be *"Dog's best friend"*.

Any dog can be a *"best friend"* to a human, providing that we humans educate ourselves and put in the work. This is a universal truth that applies to any canine breed, including the active, tenacious and intelligent Staffordshire Bull Terrier .

PERSONAL EXPERIENCE: *Many times, I've been asked to come and correct "problems" in a family that has decided to share their lives with an energetic Terrier. They show me many pictures of destruction including an excavated back yard, chewed coffee tables and more and expect me to "fix" their unruly dog that is also disturbing the neighbours with their constant barking. In every instance, the poor dog is being blamed for being a sad, lonely, highly stressed and bored captive that needs something interesting to do, much more daily exercise, and just wants to be with his or her humans.*

Rather than putting the blame where it rightfully lies, the humans expect their smart and energetic dog to be happy living alone within the walls of a house while the family is away at work all day. Again, my pet peeve (no pun intended) flairs as I am forced to tell these people that what they have asked this dog to endure is just plain cruelty, and the all-day barking or itemized destruction is NOT the dog's fault.

While the dog is willing to change right away when they get what they need, for us humans it's a long road to set this type of situation right, and sadly many of us simply don't have what it takes or are not willing to admit that we have caused the problem. What follows can often be another dog abandoned and placed behind bars at the local SPCA. Choose wisely and please don't let this ever be your story.

If you're considering this smart, highly loyal dog for your family, be absolutely certain that you are aware of their past history, and are able to involve him or her in interesting vigorous daily routines and tasks that will engage both their body and their mind. Also, be sure that you have strong enough energy to keep this dog under firm supervision, which will involve keeping him or her at your side throughout most of the day.

Providing firm guidance for this energetic, tireless, and robust Terrier will ensure that you are raising a happy dog that never has to suffer from the stress of behavioural issues or poor health.

In a Nutshell

It's important to understand that no matter the size of your chosen canine friend, you actually need to find appropriate ways to let your dog BE a dog if you want to raise a happy and healthy companion.

While being overly protective, babying them or treating them like a fur covered child may be something YOU need, it's not what THEY need.

If you are not able to be a consistently strong leader that takes on the leadership role for the Staffy, he or she may become confused about who is the boss. Be aware that confusion about who is the alpha dog in this relationship may result in the creation of unwanted behavioural issues sooner or later in life.

Chapter 6: Every Happy Staffordshire Bull Terrier Wants Exercise

"The dog lives for the day,
the hour, even the moment."
— Robert Scott

This breed will usually require a moderate to high amount of daily physical and mental exercise, that also includes going out for 2-3 on-leash walks, walking properly at your side (without pulling) every day.

The smart Staffordshire Bull Terrier will also need space to run (or swim) freely and some challenging thinking tasks that exercise the brain. This varied combination will result in a strong bond of trust and respect between you and your dog that translates to both a healthy body and a healthy mind.

If you cannot commit to the time required to ensure your dog receives regular exercise each day, that engages both mind and body, this will soon be a very bored, overweight, unhappy, stressed dog that could develop multiple health and behaviour issues.

Minimum Daily Exercise Requirements

- A minimum of three 30 to 60 minute, on-leash, disciplined walks outdoors where they are walking calmly at your side without pulling, and paying close attention to your commands.

- A minimum of one hour running, swimming, romping and socialising with other dogs or performing an interesting canine sport.
- A minimum of 15 to 30 minutes every day teaching tricks, commands, hand signals or routines that will exercise the brain.

Once properly leash trained and heeding basic commands, the Staffordshire will also need the reward of some off-leash freedom at a securely fenced local dog park where (under your close supervision) they can run, socialise, play with other dogs or perhaps fetch a ball or Frisbee and just enjoy being a dog.

When playing fetch, be careful that you do not teach your dog to swear at you or be disrespectful. You've seen it yourself I'm sure, or at least heard it. This is when a dog has been taught by their humans to be ball or Frisbee obsessed. When the dog and human arrive at the park you can already hear the dog barking at their human to throw the ball before they are even out of the vehicle.

Don't Let the Dog Be in Charge

If you do not take the time to curb a barking habit during play, you may have to endure a noisy problem that will be irritating to you and everyone else within earshot.

The Staffy will usually love to chase a fast-moving ball or Frisbee, and when playing a game of fetch, it may take only seconds for this clever canine to teach their humans that they are in charge of the game. Literally, if you are not aware of what you are "teaching", all it may take is one slip up. Once you've made this mistake, your dog may never forget that when the ball comes out, they are in charge and correcting this may take a very long time.

Consider that your dog is excited to retrieve the ball or Frisbee, so he or she barks, and you immediately throw the desired object. Guess what? You just taught your dog to bark (or swear) at you to immediately get what they want.

To do nothing about your dog barking for what they want sends an unspoken message to him or her that you approve of this type of bossy behaviour. If you simply laugh, thinking this is such a funny scene, you will be teaching your dog to continue to swear at you. Don't go there in the first place because reversing this problem can take many long and frustrating (not to mention noisy) hours to accomplish.

Instead, be proactive, always be the leader for your dog and teach him or her what is, and what is not acceptable. When you draw a firm line in the sand and are always consistent with enforcing rules and boundaries, there will be no confusion, and you will have given your loyal companion the best opportunity for a happy and stress-free life. Teach your dog to make eye contact with YOU (not the ball or Frisbee) before you throw it.

The smart Staffy can be stubborn and wilful because they come from a working background and are used to thinking for his or herself. This makes it even more important to always be firmly consistent when teaching and enforcing rules and boundaries, which includes the proper way to greet other dogs.

Your dog needs to know that YOU are always in control of what they do and that you will <u>never</u> permit any overly boisterous activity with other dogs or any attempt to dominate, be aggressive or chase other animals without your say so.

Keeping your dog "safe" first means teaching them rules and boundaries and then always being vigilant about enforcing them. This is even more important with a breed like the Staffy, which many people are already wary of. For instance, if you are uncertain about another dog approaching, simply place yourself between your dog and the approaching dog until you are certain a friendly greeting will be the outcome.

Ideal Daily Exercise Requirements

A fully-grown Staffordshire Bull Terrier will be a playful, energetic and versatile dog with endless stamina that will excel when they receive a wide variety of fun and interesting daily mental and physical stimulation from disciplined walks, exercise, play and challenging mental games or canine sports.

This Terrier is a muscular, very powerful, agile and fast-moving companion who may display a dominant attitude toward other dogs and be standoffish with strangers, which means you will always need to be firmly in control of his or her actions.

Always tireless and eager for their next adventure at the side of their human guardian, depending on what you have the desire to teach, this dog's skills can be many.

Keep in mind that, depending on the particular dog and how you raise him or her, they will generally be more or less energetic. It's a simple formula: you are more energetic, your dog is more energetic and both of you will be healthier and happier.

I've had Terrier clients whose dogs were under-exercised, frustrated, bored, and overweight, and others whose dogs were super athletes whose days were filled with energetic athletic outdoor pursuits that kept both mind and body fit and healthy. In other words, if you're active, your dog most likely will be too.

There may be many sports and services appropriate for this strong, robust, smart and agile dog that include, but are not limited to:

- Advanced Obedience
- Agility
- Flyball
- Disc Dog
- Barn Hunt
- Rally Trials

- Trick Training
- Fast CAT
- Dock Diving
- Therapy
- Conformation Shows

This tough and fearless dog has great stamina and loves to run and retrieve fast-moving objects. Another very good way to give them the amount of exercise they really need is to train them to jog beside your bicycle. Consider training this energetic Terrier to a *"Springer Bicycle Jogger"* ***(pictured),*** so that they can receive a good amount of disciplined, vigorous exercise in a short period of time. Make sure you don't pedal too fast, never overdo it, and always carry water for your dog.

The *"Springer Bicycle Jogger"* attachment for a bicycle is an ideal and safe way to adequately exercise this dog, while still keeping them under proper control, so that they cannot chase after a bird, cat or other distraction.

The Springer easily attaches to any bicycle and the arm can be quickly removed when not needed. The large spring attaches to a harness on the dog and there is a quick release, break-away tab at the top of the rope in case the dog runs around one side of a pole while you and the bike are on the other side. As well, the large spring in this arrangement ensures that if your dog tries to lunge or chase a squirrel or other distraction, you and your bicycle will remain stable.

FACT ***While the stocky Staffordshire can be a loyal, loving and affectionate family member, some countries have banned (Germany, Switzerland, Bermuda Islands) or restricted (France, Ireland, Israel, Portugal, Romania, Singapore, Spain, USA) ownership of this breed, because (like any dog) in the wrong hands, they have the potential to become dangerously aggressive.***

Ideal Living Conditions for a Happy Staffordshire Bull Terrier

This muscular companion needs to run every day and needs the opportunity to get outside for their disciplined, on-leash walks that include socialising and participating in other interesting tasks where they get to use their brain.

Also, keep in mind that while the Staffy can sometimes be stubborn, the personality of every dog will be different and depending on their human leadership will develop traits and quirks that are unique to him or her.

How each puppy will develop will depend upon careful and conscientious breeding, temperament of the parents, the environment where they are raised and how they are trained and socialised.

The Staffordshire Bull Terrier will do best with a strong guardian that maintains firm rules and boundaries that they can respect, and he or she will respond well to fair, firm and consistent training programs involving treat-based rewards or reinforcement.

"First, I want you to make sure that my dog is still in there someplace."

Properly socialising at a young age, during the first three months of his or her life, will greatly influence this dog's adult temperament, personality and behaviour as he or she matures, and will help to prevent this dog from becoming too dominant or aggressive.

Continuing to shape the personality of this dog through adolescence and on into adulthood with a combination of socialising, training, plenty of exercise, and firm rules and boundaries, will help to ensure a trustworthy, well-mannered fur friend.

If you are unable to commit to providing an appropriate routine for this robust dog on a daily basis, that includes on-going socialisation, training, mental games, and spending as much time as possible engaged in vigorous outdoor pursuits each day, this strong and athletic dog will very likely become unhealthily overweight, may become wary around other dogs that can lead to aggression, and he or she may become depressed.

An under-exercised Terrier will soon become fat, bored and unhappy, which can then cause them to develop behavioural problems that could include acting out in destructive ways by chewing "off limits" items in the home, digging holes in the garden, escaping the back yard, excessive barking, and ultimately suffering from anxiety and stress that can prematurely cause health issues and shorten their life.

Above all else, never forget that all dogs (no matter their size) are pack animals, which means that it is not normal for them to spend long periods of time in lonely isolation. This is even more important with a highly loyal and affectionate dog that comes from a working background, such as the Staffordshire Bull Terrier that needs more consistent contact with their humans.

Always remember that when you adopt a dog into your family you become their pack and you cannot simply abandon them, and forget about their needs when it's convenient for you to do so.

In other words, if you're planning to leave your Staffy alone for many hours every day, while you're at work or out for an evening at the pub with friends, perhaps you're not yet ready for the change in lifestyle that comes hand in hand with being the ideal dog guardian.

Dogs that are left alone too much often develop separation anxiety, a depressed, aggressive and unhappy state of mind, destructive tendencies and angry neighbours should your dog spend his or her lonely hours barking up a storm.

<u>In a Nutshell</u>

The bottom line here is that the Staffordshire Bull Terrier is a very strong, athletic, smart, and loyal dog that likes to work while in the close company of their humans. This dog has endless stamina and NEEDS a strong leader and plenty of interesting and fun activity to keep them happy and contented every day.

So, even before you bring him or her home, start thinking about your ability to be a strong leader, the importance of early and on-going socialisation, firm training and consistent enforcement of rules and boundaries. Once you've got all of this in hand, then it will be time to consider involving this dog in Advanced Obedience, Trick Training, Barn Hunt, Dock Diving, Flyball, Agility, and many other canine sports, that should be in the future for this highly capable fur friend.

This Chapter suggests many different canine sports that this versatile dog may naturally excel at. Truly consider involving him or her in a sport, because this is a great way to provide them with the exercise they need in a disciplined way that will engage their mind while keeping them slim and trim.

These types of activities will help to establish a firm bond of trust and respect between you, and ensure that your dog is a healthy and happy family member, while also teaching them that you are their strong leader that they must always follow without question.

Chapter 7: Feeding the Happy Staffordshire Bull Terrier

"I feel sorry for people who don't have dogs.
I hear they have to pick up food they drop on the floor."
— Unknown

A properly fed dog means a healthy, happy and longer-lived companion, so make sure that you spend an appropriate amount of time to research high-quality food and treats that will be the best for your muscular canine athlete and don't overfeed.

DID YOU KNOW? ***This dog may have a strong tendency to overeat. If there is food around, they may not know when to stop, so be careful not to overfeed or leave food items within their reach.***

We are what we eat, and the same is absolutely true for our canine companions. Make sure that you don't get into the habit of *"doctoring"* their food bowl with your human food. If you do, your dog may soon refuse to eat their doggy dinner. Don't worry, though, because even a picky eater (which is highly unlikely with this breed) will not starve him or herself, and if they refuse their expensive dog dinner tonight, so long as you don't cave, they WILL be hungry tomorrow.

First, remember that our canine friends are carnivores, which means that they derive their energy and nutrient requirements and maintain their health by consuming a diet consisting mainly or exclusively of the flesh of animal tissues. In other words, your dog is a meat eater.

Many dog guardians are unaware of the importance of feeding their dog a high-quality dog food and often make the mistake of shopping for dog food by price alone. The problem with this method is that the cheaper the dog food is, the less nutritious the quality.

Inexpensive dog food brands use low-quality fillers (wheat, corn, soy) and other unnecessary ingredients to add bulk to the product, rather than providing any nutritional benefit. Without a healthy, high-quality, balanced diet, your dog may not live as long as he or she could because poorly chosen food may lead to the development of health problems.

When choosing an appropriate diet for your Staffordshire Bull Terrier, considering the physiology of the canine's teeth, jaws and digestive tract may help to provide you with a better insight into what food your dog should be eating.

Teeth, Jaws, and Digestive Tract

Teeth: canine teeth are all sharp and pointed because they are designed to rip, shred and tear into animal meat and bone. An adult dog has on average a third more teeth than his or her human guardian.

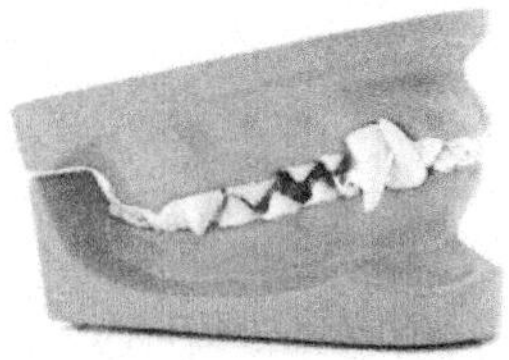

Adult canines have 42 permanent teeth in comparison to our measly 32 human teeth (without counting any wisdom teeth, which are a "bonus"). On average, puppies have 28 baby teeth, while human babies will possess 20 "baby" teeth. Puppies begin to lose those sharp baby teeth at approximately 12 to 16 weeks of age. By four months of age, almost all of a puppy's baby teeth will have been shed and been replaced by the permanent adult teeth.

Jaws: every dog is born equipped with powerful jaws and neck muscles for the specific purpose of being able to pull down and tear apart their hunted prey.

The jaw of every canine opens widely to hold large pieces of meat and bone, while the actual mechanics of the jaw permits only vertical (up and down) movement that is designed for crushing.

Digestive Tract: the canine digestive tract is short, simple and designed to move their natural choice of food (hide, meat and bone) quickly through their systems.

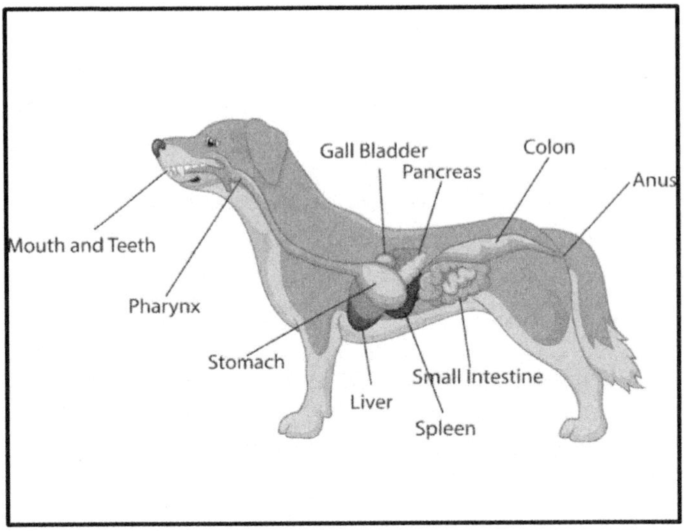

We humans need vegetables and plant matter in our diet and have the flat molars to effectively crush and chew them. While we often believe our dogs require the same, when choosing an appropriate food source for your Staffordshire, you need to consider that vegetables and plant matter require more time to break down in the gastrointestinal tract. This in turn, requires a more complex digestive system that the canine body simply does not have.

The dog's digestive system is unable to effectively break down vegetable matter, which is why whole vegetables look pretty much the same going into your dog, as they do coming out the other end.

Consider how much healthier and longer-lived your beloved Staffy might be if, instead of largely ignoring nature's design for our canine companions, we chose to feed them whole, unprocessed, species-appropriate food.

Whatever you decide to feed your dog, keep in mind that, just as too much wheat or other grains and fillers in our human diet are having detrimental effects on our human health, the same can be very true for our dogs.

Get into the habit of carefully reading labels so that you can be certain to avoid unbalanced foods that contain fillers or high amounts of grains, because these are inappropriate for a healthy canine diet.

Also consider that even though dogs ARE carnivores, some do very well on a "plant based" diet simply because our meat sources are so often polluted with wheat, chemicals, drugs and other products that would not be part of a wild dog's natural diet.

As an example, one of the world's longest living canines was a highly energetic Border Collie who was fed a clean plant-based diet, and lived to be over 25 years of age, even though average for this breed is 14.

Control of Your Happy Staffordshire Bull Terrier's Food

While some dogs may be picky eaters, and some may have a moderately healthy appetite, others can be voracious eaters. The robust and muscular Staffordshire most likely falls into the "voracious" category, and because they are deep chested, if they wolf down their food, they can suffer from life-threatening bloat. ***You will most likely want to get this dog a slow feeder type of bowl to slow them down.***

Any dog can get bored with eating the same food every day, so mix it up a little. For instance, my dog, Boris, usually had little interest in food during the morning, but was always ready for his dental treat at high noon. His internal clock was spot on and if I wasn't paying attention to the time, he would just calmly sit there staring at me until I got it.

It's important that your dog understands that YOU are in control of their food source. Once they understand this, they will also figure out that there will be windows of opportunity for receiving and eating their food, and this routine will help to develop healthy eating habits.

Many people use a scoop or measuring cup to put dry food into their dog's bowl. Why this may be a mistake is because it's very important to mix your dog's food with your hands, so that your scent is all over the food, before you offer it to them to eat. This sends a subliminal "message" to your dog that you are their pack leader, because it mimics what would happen if you were the alpha dog out hunting for your food in the wild.

For instance, while a pack of wild dogs hunting for food all work hard to capture their prey, the alpha pack leader always gets to eat first while all the other dogs must patiently wait until the leader of the pack eats their fill, before they can rush in to eat what is left over.

Therefore, when you mix your domesticated dog's dinner with your hands, you will be sending them the subtle message that you are their pack leader, you've already eaten your fill and you are now allowing them to eat what is left over.

Nutritional Needs of the Staffordshire Bull Terrier

Another crime that only CSI could solve.

Before you go shopping for dog food take the time to learn the basics about the nutritional needs of your particular fur friend. Dogs are primarily carnivorous animals, which means that most of their nutritional needs should come from animal sources – including meat, fish, and eggs.

Your dog needs a balance of protein and fat in their diet, plus healthy carbohydrates that can provide energy, fibre and other essential nutrients. It's important that your dog's daily food intake provides for their basic nutritional needs, because this is what he or she will be eating most of the time.

If you want to get into the specifics, know that protein is the most important nutrient for a dog and is required for healthy puppy growth and development. When your puppy grows up, protein will help him or her maintain lean muscle mass, so they do not become overweight or obese. Your puppy needs at least 22% protein in their diet and an adult dog needs 18%.

Next to protein, the most important nutrient for dogs is fat. While you may think of fat as a bad thing, it's actually an essential part of a balanced diet for dogs. Fat provides a concentrated source of energy and it helps your dog absorb and utilize fat-soluble vitamins. Fat should come from healthy animal sources such as chicken fat or salmon oil and should make up at least 8% of your young dog's diet. An adult dog will require a minimum of 5%.

Technically speaking, while dogs do not have specific requirements for carbohydrate in their diet, carbs can provide energy as well as fibre and other nutrients.

What you also need to remember is that your dog's body is not optimized for digesting and absorbing nutrition from plant products as much as from animal products, which means that carbohydrates in your dog's diet should be limited. They should also come from easily digestible sources such as whole grains, starchy vegetables, beans, or legumes.

Choosing a High-Quality Dog Food Brand

When shopping for food for your dog, take the time to carefully read the information on the package so that you can determine the quality of the product.

Also, if you're going to make comparisons between different products, there are three specific things to look for on the label.

(1) AAFCO Statement of Nutritional Adequacy

First, look for the Association of American Feed Control Officials (AAFCO) statement of nutritional adequacy. This is an organization that sets and upholds standards for pet food and animal feed. If you and your dog live in the United Kingdom, check for information from the Food Standards Agency (FSA).

Before a product lands on the shelf, these organizations examine it to make sure it meets the minimum nutritional requirements for the intended animal, which, in this case, is your dog. If the product is nutritionally balanced for dogs, you will see a statement like this somewhere on the label:

"[Product Name] is formulated to meet the nutritional levels established by the AAFCO Dog Food Nutrient Profiles."

If you see this on the package, you can rest assured that it will meet your dog's minimum nutritional needs. Keep in mind, however, that the AAFCO statement does not guarantee quality – you still have to read the ingredients list noted on the package to determine whether or not the product is actually a nutritious choice for your dog.

(2) Guaranteed Analysis

After the AAFCO statement, look at the guaranteed analysis – this tells you the percentages of protein, fat, fibre and moisture contained in the product. You can use the guaranteed analysis to make a direct comparison between products using those minimum values from the last section. Because your dog is better able to digest meat than plant foods, look for products that keep the fibre content less than 5%.

(3) Ingredients List

After checking the guaranteed analysis, the final place to look is the ingredients list.

The ingredients list is ordered in descending order by volume, which means that the ingredients at the top of the list are used in the highest quantity, which is the same for packages of food that you eat. You will want to see healthy, high-quality ingredients at the beginning of the list, starting with a source of animal protein. Dogs are carnivores, which means that their bodies are better able to digest and absorb nutrition from animal sources. Quality sources of animal protein for dogs include poultry, meat, and seafood.

Aside from proteins, fats, and carbohydrates, there are some other beneficial ingredients you can look for. Supplemental vitamins and minerals can improve your dog's health, because they help to protect the immune system and ensure that your dog's specific nutritional needs are met.

DID YOU KNOW? ***Synthetic supplements are not as good for your dog as natural sources for the same nutrients – such as fresh fruits and vegetables. When it comes to mineral supplements, chelated minerals are ideal – these are minerals that have been bound to protein molecules, which make them easier for your dog's body to utilize. If you see "dried fermentation products" on the list, do not be alarmed – these are probiotics that can support your dog's digestion.***

Feeding Tips

- Feeding amounts for canines vary based on factors such as breed, lifestyle, body condition and daily exercise.
- While feeding suggestions are provided on all dog food packaging, your vet may be the best resource for educating you about exactly how much you should be feeding your dog. Refer to the next section for generic feeding amount guidelines.
- Consult your vet regularly about your puppy's weight as achieving and maintaining an ideal weight not only reduces many health risks, but can also help your puppy enjoy a more energetic, longer and healthier life.

- Do not overfeed! Numerous studies indicate that dogs whose diets were responsibly restricted early on experienced longer lifespans and later onset of problems such as osteoarthritis.
- If you give your dog the occasional treat or if you use treats for training, always remember to take this into account and reduce their daily food allowance accordingly.
- As a rule of thumb, treats shouldn't make up more than 10% of your dog's daily calorie intake as this can unbalance his or her diet.
- Although it's tempting and convenient to feed your puppy table scraps, human food scraps do not provide your pup with the correct balance of nutrients.
- A puppy or adult dog rarely says no to food, but that does not mean they are always hungry. Constantly giving them food can lead to unwanted behaviour problems such as "begging for food" and hyper activity whenever they see you eating. Dogs are hard wired to always be foraging and looking for food and no matter how much you feed them, they will still ask for more. Therefore, make sure you don't let them develop this bad habit of begging for food.

- Any time you change your dog's diet, be sure to mix a little of the old food with the new food to transition them slowly as this will help to prevent digestive upset.

- If you mix your dog's food properly and he or she is still having digestive issues, it could be something else – such as food allergies.
- Food allergies affect dogs in a different way than they affect humans. While you might feel nauseous or sick after eating something you are allergic to, your dog will be more likely to develop skin problems, or throw up what they just ate.
- Red, itchy, and inflamed skin is a common sign of food allergies.
- Technically, your dog can develop an allergy to any food he or she eats, but there are some ingredients more likely to trigger food allergies in dogs than others.
- Some of the most common food allergens for dogs include beef, chicken, dairy, lamb, fish, corn, eggs, wheat, and soy, and this is usually because they came from food sources that are not "clean" or "organic". For instance, unless the chosen food is certified organic, grass fed, and contains no harmful additives, there are hidden components that can cause allergic responses. Crops such as corn, soy or wheat are often sprayed with chemicals and fed to farmed animals to fatten them up. This means that your dog may not be allergic to beef, but may be allergic to the wheat, soy or corn that was sprayed with chemicals that's been fed to the animals.
- If you suspect that your dog is suffering from a food allergy, you may need to put him or her on an elimination diet for 12 weeks or until all signs of the allergy have disappeared. At that point you can either keep feeding the elimination diet or switch to a food that doesn't contain the suspected allergen.

Feeding Puppies

A general rule of thumb for growing Staffordshire Bull Terrier puppies is to feed daily amounts of between 2 and 3% of what the puppy's adult weight is projected to be or 10% of the puppy's current body weight. You will want to keep in mind that while all puppies require extra protein to help them develop into healthy adult dogs, this is especially important with muscular, higher energy puppies.

You will also want to keep a close eye to make sure that your puppy is eating and drinking enough throughout the day, so set regular feeding times each day. The smaller the puppy, the more important this will be.

There are now many foods on the market that are formulated for all stages of a dog's life (including the puppy stage). Whether you choose one of these foods or a food specially formulated for puppies, they will need to be fed smaller meals more frequently throughout the day (between 3 and 5 times), until they are at least one year of age.

As your puppy is growing, he or she requires more nutrients and calories than an adult dog, which is the reason why puppy foods contain higher levels of protein and fat to support growth, as well as some added nutrients, such as DHA, an omega fatty acid found in mother's milk.

Once your puppy reaches adulthood, he or she will not need as many calories. Unless they are highly active, continuing to feed rich puppy food to an adult dog may quickly lead to excessive weight gain, which means that the transition to adult food is important.

TIP ***Staffordshire Bull Terrier s can be considered adults after about a year. While he or she may still be growing after this time, at the 12-month mark you can begin feeding your dog adult food.***

Feeding Adults

Choose foods that list high-quality meat protein as the main ingredient and, depending on your dog's particular energy level, feed between 2 and 3% of their body weight every day. While some dogs prefer one meal a day, most will appreciate morning food (after a walk) and evening food (after a walk).

Be careful not to get caught up in "convenience" when you're out grocery shopping for yourself, and decide to buy your dog's food at the same place, because most grocery stores tend to carry inferior brands of dog food.

Instead, make the time to visit your local pet store, talk with educated representatives, avoid grains and other fillers, and choose quality sources of meat protein for healthy puppies and dogs, including beef, buffalo, chicken, duck, fish, hare, lamb, ostrich, pork, rabbit, turkey, venison, or any other source of wild meaty protein.

Treats

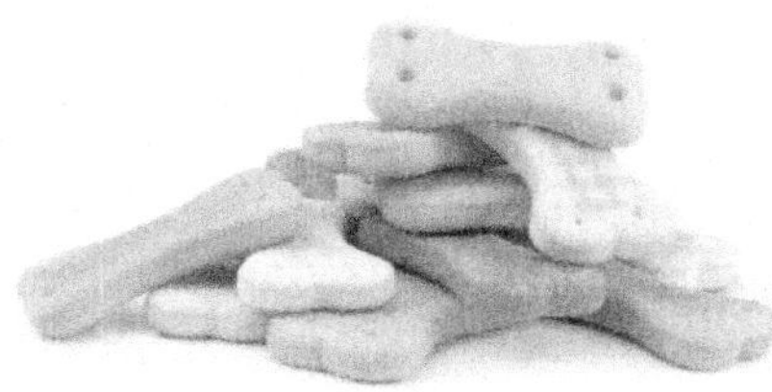

There are endless choices of dog treats lining the shelves of every feed store, pet store, and grocery store, and it will be an overwhelming task to choose wisely, unless you keep one simple rule in mind, and choose treats that contain only one ingredient or very few ingredients.

Whatever reason you choose to give treats to your dog, keep in mind that if we treat our dogs too often throughout the day, they can become overweight, and we may create a picky eater who will no longer want to eat their regular meals. Think about it – if you got to eat only your favourite tasty treats throughout the day, would you be excited about consuming a less flavourful meal come dinner time?

DID YOU KNOW? ***Researchers in Sweden have discovered that dogs were happier when they had to earn their treats as a reward for completing a task, rather than just being given a treat for looking cute, because just like us humans who get that happy "eureka" moment when we finally solve a problem, the same is true for our canine counterparts.***

The Staffy is the perfect dog for positive training methods that involve treat reinforcement.

Dangerous Treats

Always carefully read labels and take note of where treats are manufactured, because not all countries have the most stringent manufacturing protocols, and honestly there are many treats that you absolutely should NOT be feeding to your dog even though he or she may like them, including:

Rawhide (pictured) is soaked in an ash/lye solution to remove every particle of meat, fat and hair and then further soaked in bleach to remove remaining traces of the ash/lye solution. Now that the product is no longer technically food, it no longer has to comply with food regulations.

The wet rawhide is shaped into chews, and once dry it shrinks to approximately 25% of its original size before arsenic-based products are used as preservatives, and antibiotics and insecticides are added to kill bacteria.

While rawhide chews are tough and long lasting, when a dog chews a rawhide treat, they ingest many harsh chemicals. Also, when your dog swallows a piece of rawhide, that piece can swell up to four times its size inside your dog's stomach, which can cause anything from mild to severe gastric blockages that could become life threatening and require emergency surgery.

As much as it might be convenient for you to be able to give your dog or puppy a treat that will occupy them for a considerable time, if it's rawhide, just say "NO".

Pig's Ears (pictured) are very attractive to most dogs that will eagerly devour them, and they're "natural" because they're ears, so what could be wrong? Actually, these are thin, crispy and very high in fat, which can cause stomach upsets, vomiting and diarrhoea. In addition, sharp pieces can break off and become stuck in a dog's throat or cause perforations in the mouth, throat or digestive tract.

Also, pig ears are often processed and preserved with unhealthy chemicals that discerning dog guardians will NOT want to feed their dogs. Just say "NO".

Hoof Treats (pictured) are actual cow, bison, horse and pig hooves that humans believe are healthy, *"natural"* treat choices for their dogs when the truth is that after processing with harsh chemicals, preservatives and antibiotics, they retain little, if any, of their *"natural"* qualities.

Also, hooves are very hard and can cause the chipping or breaking of your dog's teeth as well as perforations in the mouth, throat or intestines, or blockages in your dog's intestines. Again, just say "NO".

Healthy Treats

As there are so many healthy treat choices available, honestly there's no excuse for feeding your dog unhealthy, toxic, nutrient-deficient or dangerous treats that could harm them. Read the labels to make sure the treats you are choosing are appropriately sized for your dog and are of the highest quality. Examples of healthy treats include:

Hard Treats: come in many varieties of shapes, sizes and flavors and will help to keep your dog's teeth cleaner.

Soft Treats: are also available in endless varieties and flavors, suitable for all the different needs of our furry friends and are often smaller in size and used for training purposes.

Dental Treats or Chews (pictured): are designed with the specific purpose of helping your dog to maintain healthy teeth and gums by exercising the jaw and massaging gums, while removing plaque build-up near the gum line.

The very best thing you can do for your dog's oral hygiene is to brush his or her teeth every day or two. However, dog dental chews can be an excellent top-up between brushing or for dogs who will not let you get anywhere near their teeth without a great struggle.

Dental chews come in both edible and non-edible varieties and lots of dogs love the taste of these chews and think of them as a tasty treat. Non-edible chews are a bit like toys for many dogs and satisfy their natural urge to chew while helping to clean their teeth at the same time.

Freeze-Dried and Jerky Treats (pictured): offer a tasty morsel most dogs find irresistible as they are usually made of simple, meaty ingredients, such as liver, poultry and seafood. Be careful when choosing jerky treats, as they are often processed with too much salt.

Human Food Treats: be very careful when feeding human foods to your dog as treats, because many of our foods contain unhealthy additives, such as salt, sugar and other ingredients that could be toxic and harmful.

Also, educate yourself about the common human foods that are actually poisonous to our canine friends, such as grapes, raisins, onions and chocolate, to name a few.

Generally, the treats you feed your dog should not make up more than approximately 10% of their daily food intake, so make sure the treats you choose are high quality, with single or few ingredients so that you can help to keep your dog both happy and healthy.

The Right Food for Your Happy Staffordshire Bull Terrier

"Dog Food" has significantly changed since1785, when the English Sportman's Dictionary described the best diet for a dog's health in an article entitled *"Dog"*. This article indicated that the best food for a dog was something called *"Greaves"*, described as "*the sediment of melted tallow made into cakes for dogs' food*".

From these meager beginnings, commercially manufactured dog food has become a massively lucrative industry that has only fairly recently evolved beyond feeding our dogs the dregs of human leftovers, because it was cheap and convenient for us.

Even today, the majority of dog food choices often have far more to do with being convenient for humans to store and serve, than it does with being a diet truly designed to be a nutritionally balanced, healthy food choice for our canine companions.

Educating yourself by talking to experts and reading everything you can find on the subject, plus taking into consideration several relevant factors, will help to answer the dog food question for you and your dog.

For instance, where you live may dictate what sorts of foods you have access to, while other factors to consider will include the particular requirements of your dog, such as their age, energy and activity levels.

Our dogs are also suffering from many of the same life-threatening diseases that are commonly found in our human society (heart disease, cancer, diabetes, obesity). These diseases all have a direct correlation with over-feeding and/or eating genetically altered foods that are no longer pure, in favour of a convenient, processed and packaged diet that is quick and easy for us to serve.

The Raw Diet: raw feeding advocates believe that the ideal diet for their dog is one which would be very similar to what a dog living in the wild would have access to while hunting or foraging.

These canine guardians are often opposed to feeding their dog any sort of commercially manufactured pet foods, because they consider them to be poor substitutes, and for the most part, I would agree.

For instance, many guardians of high energy, working breed dogs will agree that their dogs thrive on a raw or BARF (Biologically Appropriate Raw Food) diet and strongly believe that the potential benefits of feeding a raw dog food diet are many, whether your dog is earning a daily working wage or simply being your loyal companion, including:

- Healthy, shiny coats
- Decreased shedding
- Fewer allergy problems
- Healthier skin

- Cleaner teeth
- Fresher breath
- Increased energy levels
- Improved digestion
- Smaller stools
- Strengthened immune system
- Increased mobility in arthritic pets
- Increase or improvement in overall health

A raw diet is a direct evolution of what dogs ate before they became our domesticated pets and we turned toward commercially prepared, easy-to-serve dry dog food that required no special storage or preparation.

The Dehydrated Diet (pictured): is available in both raw and cooked meat forms, which are usually air dried to reduce moisture and inhibit bacterial growth. While the appearance of dehydrated dog food is very similar to dry kibble, the typical feeding methods include adding warm water before serving, which makes this type of diet both healthy for our dogs and convenient for us to serve.

Dehydrated recipes are made from minimally processed fresh, whole foods to create a healthy and nutritionally balanced meal that retains more of the overall nutritional value, and will meet or exceed the daily dietary requirements of a healthy canine.

A dehydrated diet is a convenient way to feed your dog a nutritious diet, because all you have to do is add warm water and wait five minutes while the food re-hydrates so your dog can enjoy a warm meal.

The Kibble Diet (pictured): there is no mistaking that the convenience and relative economy of dry dog food kibble, which had its beginnings in the 1940's, continues to be the most popular food choice for many dog-friendly humans. Thankfully, there are now many high-quality kibble foods available.

The Right Bowl for the Staffordshire Bull Terrier: there are many different types and categories of dog bowls, including Automatic Watering, Elevated, Ceramic, Stoneware, No Skid, No Tip, Slow Feeder, Stainless, Wooden and Travel Bowls.

Always purchase bowls that are appropriately sized for your particular dog, and consider an elevated dining table **(pictured)** so that their head is up from the floor and they can be more comfortable when eating and drinking.

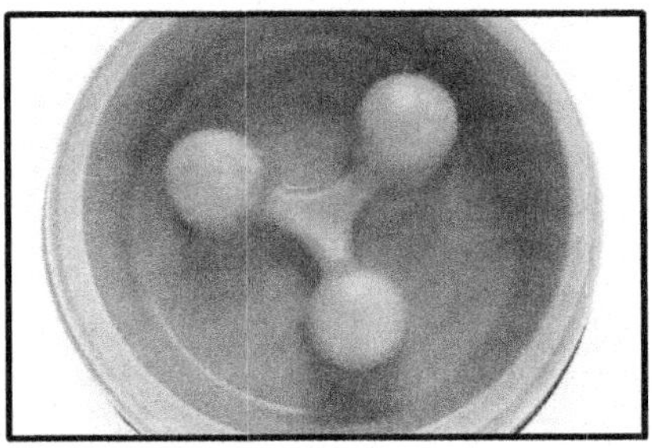

Also, if your dog wolfs their food, or has a deep chest (like the Staffordshire), consider a slow feeder type of bowl **(pictured)** to help slow down the speed at which they consume their food, so that they are not at risk for life-threatening bloat.

In a Nutshell

While making wise choices about food and treats for your favourite furry friend can be overwhelming, understanding basic canine physiology and all the many different types of food and treats available, will help add many healthy and happy years to your dog's life.

You are the sole provider and protector of your canine companion, and I cannot stress strongly enough the importance of a well thought out choice when deciding what brand and type of food and treats you will feed your loyal fur friend.

Appropriate food/treat choices and being careful to not overfeed, may not only increase the length of your dog's life by avoiding unwanted health conditions, such as allergies, obesity, high blood pressure or bladder stones, good food choices will also provide your dog with optimal health so they can feel good and live a happy life!

Chapter 8: Care of the Happy Staffordshire Bull Terrier

"When you adopt a dog, you have a lot of very good days, and one very bad day."
— W. Bruce Cameron

Imagine you're travelling by vehicle on a daily basis without being protected by a seatbelt or an airbag. Would you feel safe? Roaming about inside a moving vehicle is the reality for far too many of our furry friends, because we humans often forget to think about vehicle safety for our dogs.

Now, imagine going for months without brushing your teeth, cutting your nails, or washing your hair. This is another reality for many dogs, because their human guardians are not aware of how important it is to keep their canine fur friends well groomed. How happy and comfortable do you think such an ill cared for dog would be?

The following few paragraphs outline safe travelling, licensing, insurance and grooming requirements, all of which can help to ensure that your Staffordshire is safe, legal, better cared for at the vet's office and is well groomed.

Keep in mind that if your dog is safely secured when travelling, they might not be dead or seriously injured should you be involved in a vehicle accident. We humans wear seatbelts to be safe and we need to think about safety for our best fur friends, too.

Further, if your dog is properly licensed, they will be returned to you should they go missing, and this is a much happier dog than one spending who knows how long behind bars at a rescue or SPCA.

As well, if you have pet health insurance, chances are that your dog will be better cared for at the vet's office, because you won't have to worry about whether or not you can afford to take them, and this will most likely mean a healthier companion.

When your dog is regularly groomed, their coat and skin will look and feel better, and they won't suffer from tooth problems or sore joints from nails that are too long.

Tips for Keeping Your Dog Safe

Not So Safe Harness Restraints: is your canine companion safe when buckled into a safety harness for travel in vehicles? Be aware that many of the dog harnesses in the marketplace have a 100% failure rate.

If you are unable to find a safety harness that has actually been strength and crash tested (i.e. optimal choice), the safest travel arrangement for any dog is to secure them inside a kennel, that is bolted to the floor or secured with the vehicle's seatbelt system.

Remember that a dog travelling in the front passenger seat, even one secured with a proper safety harness, may still sustain injuries (and even death) if the 100 mph force of the airbag strikes them.

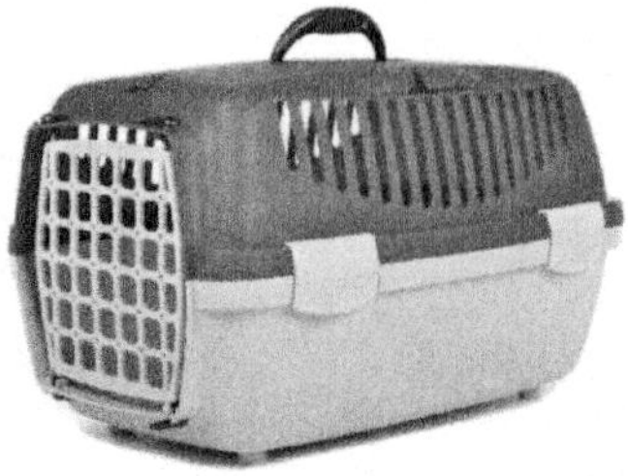

Kennels: a dog kennel or crate will easily fit on the back seat of most vehicles and can be secured with the vehicle's restraint system. A Staffy (or any dog) riding inside a kennel that is secure inside your vehicle will have the best protection in the case of a rollover accident, plus you will avoid the fines some locations are now levying because permitting a dog to freely roam about inside a moving vehicle is considered a distraction that can cause an accident.

Air Travel: while the Staffordshire puppy may be small enough to fit into a soft Sherpa bag for travel inside an airplane cabin (as carry-on baggage), he or she will definitely be too large when they attain their adult size. Any puppies or dogs that are too large to fit comfortably inside a Sherpa travel bag will need to be transported inside a heated cargo hold.

Licensing: when you purchase your dog a yearly license, and you attach this identifying tag to their collar, they will be legal. Any dog that should become lost when wearing a license will have a much higher possibility of being returned to you, instead of spending their last few days behind bars at the local SPCA or rescue facility.

Pet Health Insurance: purchasing health insurance for your dog means that they will usually live a longer, healthier and happier life, because they will receive better and often more frequent care throughout their lifetime.

TIP ***Be aware that it's a better idea to begin insurance when your dog is a young puppy, because waiting until they are older will mean that your monthly premiums will be considerably higher.***

Puppy Proofing

As a dog owner, it will be your responsibility to make sure that your Staffordshire's needs are taken care of, and this all begins with prepping your home for a new puppy by puppy-proofing to keep him or her safe.

Next, you will need to learn what and how often to feed your puppy and when to transition them to an adult dog food formula (previous chapter). You will also need to take care of your dog's grooming requirements, which is discussed later on in this chapter.

When it comes to preparing your home for a new dog, you will need to do some puppy proofing. Start by walking through your home and try to view it through a puppy's eyes to identify potential dangers. Here's a list of some of the things you may need to do:

- Store cleaning products where your puppy cannot reach them or put them in a locked cabinet.

- Put all trash in a can with a tight-fitting lid or keep it secured in a cupboard.
- Store open food containers in your pantry or cupboards – anything left out needs a lid.
- Tie up or bundle any electrical cords and blind cords so your puppy cannot chew on them.
- Pick up small objects from the floor – they are a choking hazard for a curious puppy.
- Cover open bodies of water (such as the toilet, bathtub, outdoor ponds, swimming pools, etc.).

- Put all medications and other toiletries where your puppy cannot reach them, such as in the medicine cabinet and use childproof bottles.
- Make sure none of your house plants or plants in your yard are toxic to dogs – if there are any suspect plants or flowers, remove them, move them out of reach, or fence them off.
- Keep your windows and doors securely closed when your puppy is roaming around – close doors, use baby gates or pet gates to keep them away from areas where you do not want them to wander.
- If you have a cat, keep the litter box where your puppy cannot reach it, so he does not eat the clumps.
- Dispose of all food waste properly so your puppy cannot get it – this is especially important for chicken bones and foods that are harmful to dogs.
- Store all lawn and garden tools where your puppy cannot get to them and make sure they will not fall over if your puppy bumps into them.
- If you have a yard, consider adding a fence to keep your puppy in.

- Never leave them alone in a back yard, because even a fenced yard is little deterrent to a motivated Staffy who is a natural digger, has no fear of heights and is smart enough to figure out how to escape.
- Avoid using toxic chemical fertilizers, pesticides, or herbicides anywhere your puppy could be exposed – this includes toxic carpet and floor cleaning products.

Once you have puppy-proofed your home, the next step is to set up your puppy's area. You can choose a small room or use a puppy playpen to cordon off a section of a larger room.

Place your puppy's crate and dog bed in the playpen area as well as their food, water bowls and toys. You will want to put your pup in this area when you cannot actively watch him or her so they are less likely to get into trouble.

While your puppy is very young, when you cannot closely watch them, such as when you need to take a shower, you may also want to confine him or her to their crate until they are housetrained.

Grooming Your Dog

Regular grooming is important for every happy and healthy dog, because it keeps them clean, and their skin moisturized and bug free, plus grooming time can alert you to any problems before they become more serious.

The Staffordshire Bull Terrier will have a short, smooth coat, which will require minimal weekly brushing to remove debris and distribute natural oils.

Hair Brushing Technique

- Use a soft bristle brush to brush out your dog's coat at least twice a week.
- Start at the base of the neck and work your way down the back and sides, always brushing in the direction of hair growth.

- Next, brush down each leg then have your dog roll over so you can brush out their underside. Don't forget the tail.

Depending upon whether you decide to fully groom your dog yourself, or will take him or her to the local doggy spa, you will require minimal equipment to keep the coat of your happy Terrier looking his or her best.

If you're just keeping on top of weekly brushing, all you will need is a soft bristle brush, and perhaps a flea comb (just in case). If you're planning to do all your dog's grooming yourself, see *"Grooming Equipment You Will Need"* on the next page.

Also, it will be very important to get this dog used to their grooming routine early on, because during their lifetime there are many grooming procedures you will need to keep on top of. Otherwise, every time your dog needs to be bathed and brushed or have their nails clipped or their teeth brushed will end up being a traumatic experience for both dog and human that can last for many years. Start them off right so you can both enjoy grooming time.

I've been asked to groom dogs that have been kicked out of every grooming salon because their owners did not take the time to introduce the puppy to bath time, nail trimming and hair clipping procedures at a young age.

I can tell you from much personal experience that having to groom a writhing, screaming dog that is all teeth, because they are fighting the procedure, is hell on wheels, and the very worst case I ever encountered was with a dog weighing only 4 pounds (1.8 kg). Try going through this with an unwilling, much more muscular and athletic Staffordshire Bull Terrier, and you will very soon be wishing your companion were a chia pet.

Grooming Equipment You Will Need

A standard arsenal of equipment for the DIY groomer that will help you keep your dog looking their best will include the following:

Soft Bristle brush (pictured) – is the ideal tool for removing dirt and debris from the Staffordshire's coat, while at the same time

distributing natural oils to keep the coat looking healthy and shiny.

Nail clippers (pictured) or a slow speed pet Dremel™ – will be tools you need to use every couple of weeks or more, depending on how quickly your dog's nails grow, their activity level and what types of surfaces they may be walking on. The pet Dremel is perfect for smoothing the sharp edges that nail clippers leave, and if you are vigilant with regular use of the Dremel, you may never have to clip.

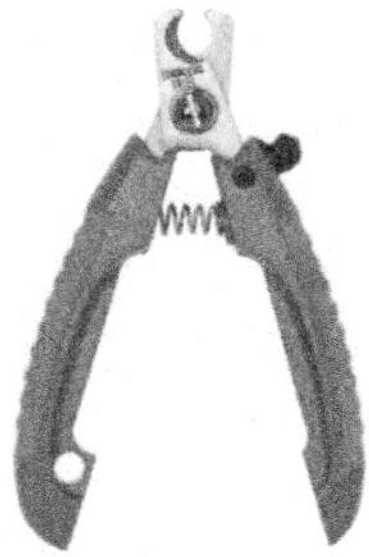

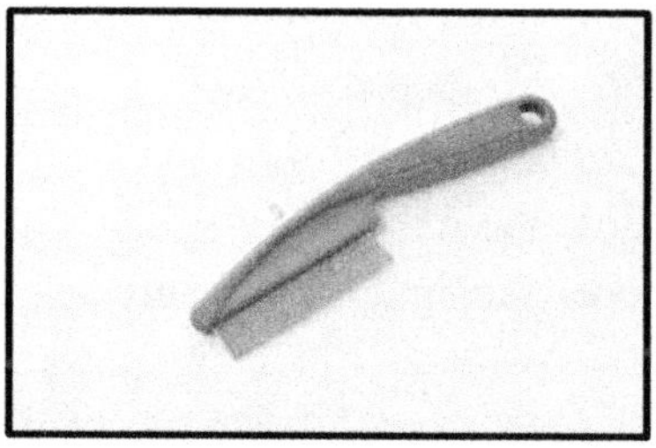

Flea comb (pictured) – while you may never need one, as the name suggests, these combs are designed for the specific purpose of removing tiny mites or fleas from a dog's coat. Usually small in size for manoeuvring in tight spaces, they are made of plastic or metal with the teeth placed closely together to trap and remove hiding pests.

Tick Twister (pictured) – hopefully your dog won't ever get a tick, but if they do, this is a simple device for painlessly, easily and quickly removing ticks that have imbedded themselves in your dog's skin.

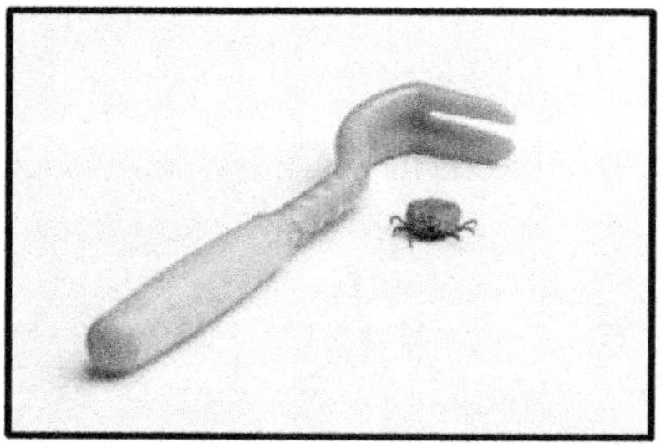

<u>Grooming Products You Will Need</u>

Products you will need to invest in when bathing your dog yourself will include shampoos, conditioners, creams, lotions, sprays and powders.

Shampoos: NEVER make the mistake of using human shampoo or conditioner that has a pH balance of 5.5, for bathing your dog. Our canine companions have an almost neutral pH balance of 7.5, and any shampoo with a lower pH will be harmful to your dog, because it will strip the natural oils and be too harshly acidic for their skin and coat, and can cause itchy skin problems that will make your dog very unhappy.

Conditioners: it's a good idea to take the extra time to condition your dog's coat because doing so will not only make it look and feel better, it will also add many additional benefits, including:

- Preventing the escape of natural oils and moisture
- Keeping the coat cleaner for a longer period of time
- Repairing a dull, damaged or dry coat
- Restoring a soft, silky feel to the coat
- Helping the coat dry more quickly
- Protection from the heat of the dryer and breakage of hair

The benefits of spending the extra two minutes to condition your dog's coat will be appreciated by both yourself and your dog that will have overall healthy, moisturized skin and a coat with a smooth feel and natural shine.

Bathing your dog:

- To bathe your dog, simply fill your bathtub with a few inches of lukewarm water and place your dog in it – you can put a bath mat or towel down to keep him or her from slipping.
- Then, use a cup or a hand sprayer to wet down your dog's coat and work a little bit of dog-friendly shampoo into a thick lather.
- Rinse the coat well until the coat is completely free of all shampoo suds, and squeeze out the excess water with your hands.
- Apply canine conditioner and then rinse the coat thoroughly before squeezing out excess water and towelling your dog dry.
- If it's a cold day, it's a good idea to use a hairdryer on a warm setting to completely dry the coat. Puppies can especially get cold quickly after a bath.
- Unless your dog gets dirty, you should only plan to bathe him or her once every 4 to 6 weeks because bathing too often can dry out your dog's skin and coat.

Oops, My Dog Has Fleas

Perhaps you haven't been paying attention and now realize that your dog is suffering from an infestation of fleas. Now is the time to bathe them with shampoo containing pyrethrum (a botanical extract found in small, white daisies) or a shampoo containing citrus, cedar or tea tree oil.

Also, you can bathe and spray them with the non-toxic and highly effective CedarCide products, which can also be used to spray down their bedding and any carpets in the home. This highly effective product will kill fleas (or other crawly creatures) on contact without harming anyone.

CedarCide is a trusted company that makes 100% safe, organic products to control biting pests on your furry friends without the worry of toxic, harmful chemicals that are not good for you, your children or your canine companions because it's safe to use on dog and human alike.

Simply spray it on and bugs of any sort that come into contact with the solution will be instantly dead, while your dog's coat will be shiny and fresh smelling, like the inside of a cedar chest.

Nail Care

Many canine guardians neglect taking regular care of their dog's toenails because we're not comfortable with the process. Leaving a dog's nails too long can lead to many problems later in life, such as painful joints, back pain and difficulty walking, which will make for a very unhealthy and unhappy dog.

Do yourself and your dog a favour, and purchase a professional pair of medium-sized, scissor-type nail clippers with a safety stop and learn how to properly use them. If you don't, your dog's nails will soon be too long and the vein inside the nail will also grow too long and you will be unable to keep them as short as they should be.

TIP ***Get your puppy used to having their nails trimmed. Purchase a pair of "nail scissors" which are much smaller and easier to handle for tinier nails, and simply snip off the sharp curved end of the nail.***

Depending on the types of surfaces your dog is walking on, you should plan to clip your dog's nails approximately every two weeks. When trimming the nails, be sure to only snip the tip. You don't want to accidentally cut into the vein, because this will be painful for your dog and will cause the nail to bleed.

Steps For Nail Clipping

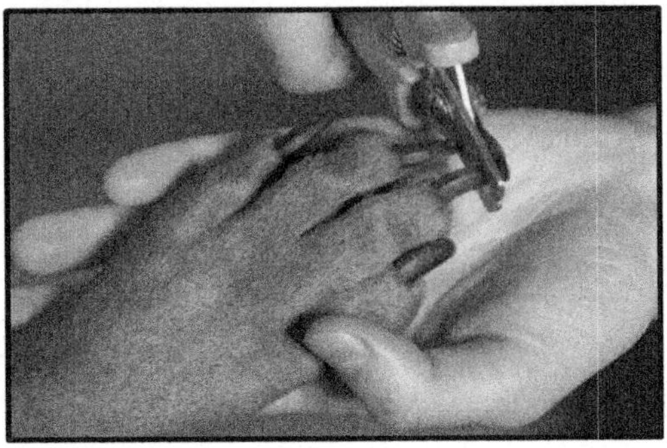

- Hold your dog's paw firmly but gently.
- Trim the nail below the quick at a 45° angle, cutting small amounts at a time.
- Trim small slices until you reach the white inside the nail with a small black dot at the centre. If you can't see the dot yet, and all you are seeing is completely white, you can cut a bit more.

If your puppy has not had their "dew claws" removed (these are the claws that are on the side of the foot that never touch the ground), they still continue to grow. If you miss clipping these nails, they will soon grow into a circle that will be very difficult to clip and can even grow back into the dog's leg causing great pain.

Styptic Powder: Of course, you will always want to avoid causing any pain when trimming your dog's toenails, because you don't want to destroy their trust in you regularly performing this necessary task.

However, sometimes accidents do happen. Therefore, if you clip too short, and accidentally cut into the vein in the toenail, know that you will cause your dog pain, and that the toenail will bleed. Therefore, it is always a good idea to keep some styptic powder (often called *"Kwik Stop")* in your grooming kit.

Dip a moistened finger into the powder and apply it with a little pressure to the end of the bleeding nail, because this is the quickest way to stop a nail from bleeding in just a few seconds.

Some dogs prefer having their nails trimmed with a rotary "Dremel" type of device that grinds down the excess nail. There are several benefits inherent in using this tool for keeping your dog's nails trimmed, including: (a) it is easier to avoid cutting into the vein; (b) many dogs prefer it because there is no squeezing or clicking sound; (c) you can smoothly round the nails so there will be no sharp edges; and (d) when you use this tool every week, you can trim shorter and will never have to actually clip the nails.

TIP ***Keep in mind that if you decide to trim your dog's nails this way, you MUST purchase a "doggy Dremel" made especially for this purpose (pictured), because using your shop Dremel will harm your dog's nails as it is too high speed and will burn the nails.***

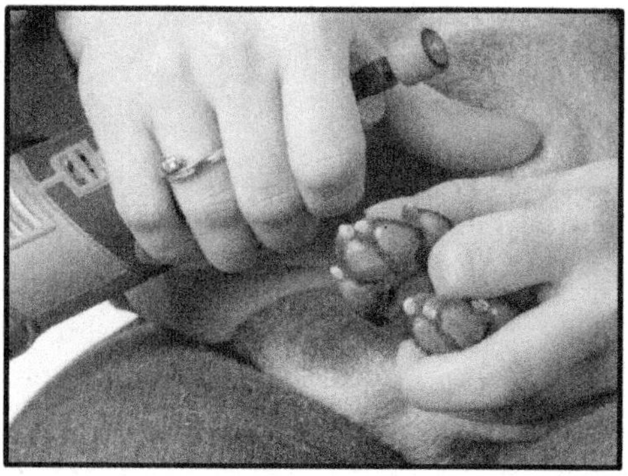

Ear Care

While dogs can often suffer from painful ear infections, paying attention and keeping your dog's ears clean and dry can go a long way toward preventing this type of unhappy health issue. If you notice your dog scratching at their ears, moaning, crying or constantly shaking their head, it's time for a trip to the vet's office. Make sure that you keep ear powders and cleaning solutions in your grooming kit, because with proper preventative care, you can help to prevent your dog from ever having to suffer from an irritating and painful ear infection.

Ear Powders: can be purchased at any pet store, and are designed to help keep your dog's ears dry while at the same time inhibiting the growth of bacteria that can lead to infections. Ear powders are also used when removing excess hair growth from inside a dog's ear canal, as the powder makes it easier to grip the hair.

Ear Cleaning Solutions: your local pet store will offer a wide variety of ear cleaning creams, drops, oils, rinses or wipes specially formulated for cleaning your dog's ears.

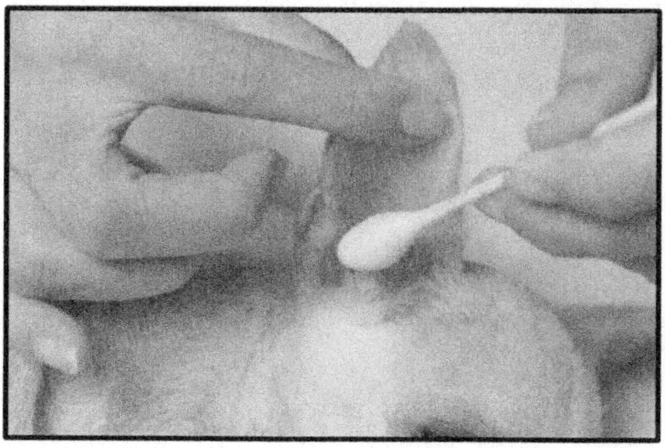

In addition, there are many home remedies that will just as efficiently clean your dog's ears without the high price tag, including Witch Hazel (a 50:50 solution of

Organic Apple Cider Vinegar and Purified Water) or a 50:50 solution of Hydrogen Peroxide and Purified Water.

Cleaning your dog's ears

- Lift your dog's ear, holding it between your thumb and forefinger to get a good look inside the ear.
- Check for redness, discharge or bad smell. It is normal to see a small amount of light-coloured wax. If there is a very large amount, the ears are red, or there appears to be pus or a bad smell, this is a sign of a problem that will require immediate veterinary attention.
- Gently wipe around the entrance of the ear canal with damp cotton wool, removing dirt or excess wax.
- Insert the tip of the bottle into the ear canal making sure not to insert it too far, and then squeeze to release the ear cleaner.
- Massage the base of the ear to help the cleaner pass inside the ear canal, and then wipe away any excess with damp cotton wool.
- Repeat the same process for the other ear.
- If there is an infection and your vet has prescribed drops, it's best to apply them straight after you've finished cleaning the ears. This will ensure that the medicine will enter the ear effectively and be absorbed without being blocked by excess wax.

Teeth Care

Another greatly overlooked area in your happy dog's health is ensuring that their teeth are clean and properly looked after, so that they don't suffer from loose or broken teeth, and plaque build-up that leads to painful gum disease. You know how miserable a toothache can be – imagine your poor dog that cannot tell you how unhappy they are.

Many guardians use the excuse that *"my dog doesn't like it"* when they try to brush their dog's teeth.

Do NOT give up and overlook the fact that in order to keep the entire dog healthy, they must have healthy teeth and the only way to ensure this, is to commit to making the time to brush your dog's teeth every day or two.

Canine Toothpastes: are flavoured with beef or chicken in an attempt to appeal to the dog's taste buds, and some contain baking soda, which is the same mild abrasive found in many human pastes, and are designed to gently scrub the teeth.

Other types of canine toothpastes are formulated with enzymes that are designed to work chemically by breaking down tartar or plaque in the dog's mouth. While these pastes don't need to be washed off your dog's teeth and are safe for them to swallow, whether or not they remain on the dog's teeth long enough to do any good might be debatable.

Just as effective for killing germs, whitening and cleaning your dog's teeth, and much less expensive than fancy pastes, is old-fashioned hydrogen peroxide; you can also combine hydrogen peroxide (3% food grade), Aloe Vera juice (1:1) with a little bit of baking soda.

How can I brush my dog's teeth?

In the beginning, it's important to get your dog used to the toothpaste and to the whole brushing experience. Here is the technique I use:

- Check your dog's teeth and gums often to see what is normal so you can spot any issues or problems.

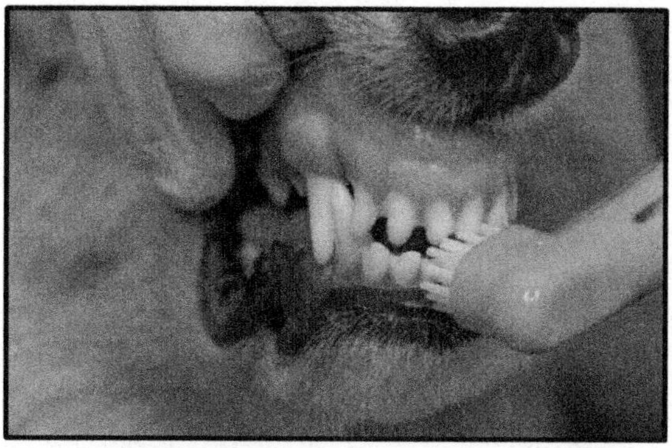

- During the first few days, hold your dog as you would normally when you are petting him or her.
- Gently stroke the outside of the cheeks with your finger for 1 or 2 minutes.
- After each session, reward your dog with praise and a treat they like. For the next few days, after your dog has become comfortable with this activity, place a small amount of toothpaste on your finger and let your dog try the flavour.

- Next, you should introduce your dog to a canine toothbrush or finger brush.
- Apply a pea-sized amount of toothpaste that has been specially formulated for dogs on the brush. Gently lift your dog's upper lip and place the brush against an upper tooth.
- With a slow circular motion, brush gently only that tooth and the adjoining gum line.
- Every following day gradually increase the number of teeth being brushed. Remember to go slowly, and do not continue beyond your dog's point of comfort.
- Build up to 30 seconds of brushing per side.
- The easiest way to do this is to go straight, pushing the brush gently from front to back along the gum line. Next, add in the gentle circular motion.
- You do not have to brush the inside of the teeth, as the tongue keeps that side relatively free of plaque.
- After each session reward your dog with a treat and lots of praise.
- Ideally, brushing should be done every day, but if you miss 1-2 days per week, that would not be a big concern.

The easiest and most effective way to brush a dog's teeth is with an electric toothbrush (the rotary type) that does all the work for you. You can easily slowly introduce this method, just as you did with the manual brush, and once your dog gets used to the buzzing, all you have to do is hold the brush against their teeth.

Paw Care

If your dog runs over sharp barnacles on the beach, jogs with you on hard road surfaces, or over other rough terrain, this can cause cuts and scrapes and very rough surfaces on the paws. If you live in a hot climate, be aware that sidewalks, road surfaces and sandy beaches can get extremely hot for your dog's feet.

Paw Creams: depending upon activity levels and the types of surfaces our canine counterparts usually walk on, they may suffer from cracked or rough pads. You can restore resiliency and keep your dog's paws in healthy condition by regularly applying a cream or lotion especially formulated for dogs that will help to protect their paw pads and a good time to do this is just after you've clipped or ground down their nails.

<u>In a Nutshell</u>

Learning a simple routine that will keep your Staffordshire Bull Terrier safe, and being aware of what's involved in keeping him or her properly groomed will go a long way toward helping them to live a long, happy and healthy life.

While for many people the concept of grooming a dog conjures up notions of brushes and bows, it is in fact a vital element to their overall health and wellbeing.

Whether you decide to bathe and clip nails yourself, or hire someone to do it for you on a regular basis, brushing your dog's teeth is an essential task that will be required every day or two.

Also, you might want to keep in mind that carrying out these essential grooming procedures yourself will strengthen the bond between you and your best fur friend and may alert you to any underlying diseases or conditions early on that could help your dog feel better.

Chapter 9: Are YOU the Ideal Happy Staffy Guardian?

"A dog is the only thing on earth that loves you more than he loves himself."
— Josh Billings

If you have not chosen wisely when sharing your life with a canine companion, he or she will not be happy and neither will you, because you will be setting yourself, your family, your friends and your neighbours up for many years of stress, guilt and unhappiness.

You may not have considered that bringing a dog into your family is a very big lifestyle change. It is vitally important that you take an honest, accurate look at your own energy level and lifestyle, ask yourself some serious questions while not scrimping on taking the time to carry out plenty of research about the breed of dog you may be considering.

Sharing your life with a canine friend should never be undertaken lightly, on a whim or spur of the moment decision, or because you like the colour of a dog's coat or the sweet expression on their face.

Do You Have What It Takes?

Before you can learn how to become your dog's best friend and ideal guardian, you need to first have no doubt in your mind that you have the energy, commitment, time and skill level necessary so that you can raise a happy dog. Once this is established in the affirmative, you then need to know how to choose the right breed of puppy or dog.

Choosing the right puppy for your family and your lifestyle is more important than you might imagine, and far too many people forget to consider how vital it is to choose a puppy or dog based on an honest assessment of compatibility with their own energy and lifestyle.

For instance, many humans choose a puppy (or older dog) for all the wrong reasons, including because:

- they like what it looks like
- the breed may currently be popular
- they like that this dog's coat is easy care
- the breed appeared on TV or in a movie they enjoyed
- their parents had the same kind of dog when they were a child
- a friend or someone they admire has the same breed
- they feel sorry for a homeless dog
- a friend or family member can no longer keep their dog
- the children are begging for a dog
- someone was selling puppies on a street corner

While some of these above reasons can be honourable, the most important reasons for choosing to share your life with a particular canine companion has not been properly considered.

In order to make an intelligent choice that will bring happiness to everyone, all you need to do is take a serious look at your life as it is today and then how you envision it to be during the next ten to fifteen years, followed by asking yourself several very important questions, including:

Activity – Do I lead a highly active, medium or low-intensity life? For instance, am I out jogging the streets every morning, hiking local mountains or riding my bicycle five miles to the local grocery store? Does my job keep me away from home, or does my leisure time activity keep me in front of the computer or on the couch watching movies?

"Can't take my dog?! But I don't even know HOW to run without my dog!"

Travel – Do I travel a lot for work or pleasure? If you do, perhaps you should choose a small dog that can travel with you in the plane cabin. Your loyal dog will be unhappy without you or you will have greatly increased expenses, because you will have to hire a dog sitter or leave them in a kennel.

Special Needs – do I have the extra finances required to keep a Staffordshire Bull Terrier well cared for? Am I able to keep this muscular, loyal dog at my side throughout most of every day? Do I have the time and fitness level to keep up with such an energetic dog?

Allergies – Do I prefer a very tidy house? Do I have allergies? This dog sheds their hair year-round and if you or a family member has allergies, the Staffordshire may not be a good choice for allergy sufferers and neat freaks.

Time – Does my family take up all my spare time and are my children old enough to handle a puppy? A dog is like a child that never grows up and in order for them to be happy and well-behaved family members, they require a LOT of your daily time and attention.

Fitness – Am I physically fit and healthy enough to be out there walking and exercising a dog two to three times a day, every day, rain or shine, and much more during the puppy stage? Do I have the time to involve this highly energetic Terrier in a canine sport and do I have a strong enough personality to keep this dog in check? Remember that this dog comes from a fighting background and needs extensive socialisation, firm training, and at least 1-2 hours of vigorous activity every day.

Cost – Am I able to afford the extra food costs, possible trips to the grooming parlour, health insurance, licensing, appropriate clothing and the veterinarian expenses that are part of being a conscientious guardian?

Commitment – Is the decision to bring a puppy or dog into my life a family decision, or just because the children, who may quickly lose interest, have been begging for a dog?

Why? – What is the number one reason why I want a dog in my life?

Once you ask yourself these important questions and honestly answer them, you will have gained a much better understanding of whether or not you have what it takes to share your life with a dog, and perhaps the beginning insight into the type of puppy or dog that would be best suited for you and your family.

If you're too busy for a dog, or choose the wrong dog that is not compatible with you or your family's energy and lifestyle (or you don't really have the time, finances, patience, expertise and commitment necessary to properly socialise, train, exercise, feed, groom, raise and care for a canine companion), you will inevitably end up with an unhappy dog. This will lead to behavioural issues, which then will lead to a stressed family, angry neighbours, and in a best-case scenario, extra expenses to hire a professional to help you reverse unwanted behavioural problems.

Even worse, an incompatible choice can mean that you may end up in a lawsuit or contributing to the already overflowing crisis of yet another dog being abandoned at the local SPCA or kill shelter.

Once you have done all your homework, and absolutely determined that the highly energetic, muscular, fearless, athletic and loyal Staffordshire Bull Terrier is the right dog for you (see next Section: The Ideal Guardian), rather than simply leaving it to chance, you need to choose the right puppy from the litter.

<u>How to Choose Your Staffordshire Bull Terrier Puppy</u>

Generally speaking, when choosing a puppy out of a litter, look for one that is friendly and outgoing, rather than one who is overly aggressive or nervous.

Visit the breeder and take note of a puppy's social skills when they are still with their littermates, because this will help you to choose the right puppy for your family. Puppies who demonstrate good social skills with their littermates are much more likely to develop into easy-going, happy adults who play well with other dogs.

When all the puppies can be observed together in a social setting, there are several important observations you can make, including:

Play – When the puppies are wrestling or play fighting, notice which puppies are comfortable both on top and on the bottom and which puppies seem to only like being on top. Puppies who don't mind the less aggressive posture of being on the bottom or who appear to be fine with either position will usually play well with other dogs when they become adults.

Sharing – Observe which puppies try to keep the toys all to themselves and which ones will share. Those who want to keep all other puppies away so that they can hoard the toys for his or herself may have tendencies to be more aggressive with other dogs when food, treats or toys are involved as they become older.

Company – Notice which puppies seem to like the company of the other pups and which ones seem to be loners. Those who like the company of their littermates are less likely to become anti-social, and more likely to be interested in the company of other dogs as they mature.

Compassion – Observe the reaction of puppies that get yelped at when they bite or roughhouse with another puppy too hard. Puppies who stop or ease up when another puppy cries or yelps in pain are more likely to respond appropriately during rough adult play.

Sociability – Is the puppy you are interested in sociable with people? If he or she will not come to you, or seems to be afraid of strangers, this may develop into a fear/aggression problem that can escalate into biting when they become adults.

Handling – Is the puppy you are interested in relaxed about being picked up or handled? A puppy that is not relaxed about being handled may become nervous or difficult around children or adults during daily interactions, when grooming is required, or when visiting the veterinarian's office.

Is Your Happy Puppy Healthy?

While mental health is very important, you will also want to do all you can to determine if your chosen puppy is physically healthy.

First, ask to see veterinarian reports from the breeder to satisfy yourself that the puppy is as healthy as possible, and then once you make your decision to share your life with a particular puppy, and they are old enough to bring home, make an appointment with your own veterinarian for a complete examination.

However, before you take your new puppy home, there are general signs of good physical health to be aware of, including the following:

Body Fat – a healthy puppy will look round and well fed, with an obvious layer of fat over their rib cage.

Breathing – a healthy puppy will breathe quietly, without sneezing, wheezing or coughing.

Coat Condition – a healthy puppy will not be itchy and will have a soft coat with no bald spots, dandruff, dullness or greasiness.

Energy Level – a well-rested puppy will be energetic and alert.

Hearing – a healthy puppy should react if you clap your hands, click your tongue or snap your fingers behind their head.

Genitals – a healthy puppy will not have any sort of discharge visible in or around their anal or genital regions.

Mobility – a healthy puppy will walk and run normally without limping, wobbling, or appearing to be stiff, sore, unstable or weak.

Vision – a healthy puppy will have bright, clear eyes without crust or discharge and they should notice if a toy is tossed nearby or a ball is rolled within their field of vision.

The Ideal Guardian Profile

Once you have established that you have what it takes to share your life with a dog (by considering the questions in the previous Section), you should consider the following tips to determine whether the Staffordshire Bull Terrier would be the right breed for you and your family.

This Terrier will be an excellent choice for high to very high-energy individuals or families who live in a large home with a yard or on a property or hobby farm, and may have children that understand how to respect a dog that has considerable mental and physical exercise needs.

This dog could be a loyal companion for active senior adults who have the knowledge to raise a strong breed and have the energy, time and mobility required to provide this muscular and athletic companion with the vigorous daily exercise and mental stimulation they need.

Keep in mind that a well-socialised dog that heeds their guardian's word will usually be accepting toward both unknown dogs and humans; when not trained to follow their guardian's lead and not adequately socialised, this fearless dog could become dominant, or aggressive in unfamiliar situations. The Staffy is not usually a dog that will back down from a fight if they feel challenged, and if you baby them too much you could be responsible for this dog developing behaviour problems.

The ideal guardian for the Happy Staffordshire Bull Terrier will be a person who is a naturally strong leader, and understands the importance of firm rules and boundaries to keep this dog in check. This person may be retired or working at home, and will enjoy several energetic daily walks plus off leash time to let their dog freely run, and ideally some time for a canine sport. This guardian will also be aware of this dog's high stamina and strong desire to work, and that they may develop depression, frustration, a nervous disposition or separation anxiety (that leads to destructive behaviour and escape attempts), if they are expected to spend long hours alone every day.

This ideal guardian will also understand the importance of early and on-going socialising, supervision and firm, fair training. This individual may also enjoy teaching their companion tricks and/or a fun canine sport, and be willing to involve him or her in their own daily walking, biking, swimming, jogging or hiking routine.

As an example, this dog's guardian may be someone who takes his or her dog out for a brisk 30-minute walk, so they can empty their bladder and bowels first thing every morning before breakfast, rain or shine, plus some off-leash time where they can run freely chasing and retrieving a ball or socialising and safely playing with other dogs.

After returning home, everyone will have their breakfast and then (since you work at home or are retired) your dog can relax on the couch for a couple of hours while you work about the home. Before long it's noon and time to leash up your companion and head off for a longer walk. Depending on the weather, you may finish up at the lake or ocean side for a game of fetch in the water. If it's a hot day out, always carry water for your dog, and don't let them play too long.

Back home for a midday dental snack for your dog and lunch for you, while you take time (depending on this dog's age) to teach basic commands, play a short game in the back yard, maybe teach some tricks, or head off to the local Agility or Flyball course.

Now it's about 4:00 pm and again it's time to get you and your dog outside for a 30-minute walk around the block, or perhaps hitch them up to a Springer bicycle jogger and let them jog beside your bicycle. Then if it's not too hot or too cold out, perhaps another short stop at the park for socialising and running free with other dogs.

TIP ***Keep in mind that if you live where the winters are harsh and you have access to a treadmill, this dog can quickly be taught to exercise indoors alongside you on a treadmill.***

Back home and time to prepare dinner for both dog and human, then after dinner (again depending on the age of your dog) perhaps a few more minutes of basic command and/or trick training before you head off to the local dog park for a game of Frisbee.

Now it's getting to be later evening and before bed you need to put your dog on leash and take them outside for a few minutes so they can drain out their bladder before bed.

Everyone now in his or her respective beds as both human and dog have a rejuvenating sleep before the start of the next day when you do this (or something similar) all over again.

Of course, this is just one scenario that would be excellent for the Happy Staffordshire Bull Terrier, and with a little imagination on your part, there are many others that would fit the bill quite nicely.

Also, don't forget to check out your local weekend canine sporting facilities, because once your Staffy is well socialised and trained to follow your lead, your weekend would be well spent teaching this robust dog how to run an Agility course, or perhaps participate in Advanced Obedience or even sniff out a pretend rat in a Barn Hunt competition.

In a Nutshell

While learning how to choose the right puppy is important, even more important is your ability to ask and honestly answer the questions outlined in this Chapter that will help you to understand if you truly are a good fit for being the ideal guardian for this imposing Terrier, who will be your devoted and loving companion for many years.

Remember that if you don't really have the time, commitment and knowledge necessary to properly socialise, train and raise this muscular and energetic companion (that includes daily mental and physical exercise), you will inevitably end up with an unhappy dog. This will lead to health and behavioural issues, which then will lead to a stressed dog, a stressed family, possibly angry neighbours, and extra expenses to hire a professional to help you reverse unwanted behavioural problems, which is, of course, only possible if YOU are willing to make the necessary changes in your life.

Chapter 10: Humans Can Make Mistakes

"Heaven goes by favor. If it went by merit,
you would stay out and your dog would go in."
— Mark Twain

Far too often we humans don't even realize we are the cause of creating behavioural problems in our canine companions. When we're not aware and paying attention, we may actually be causing issues that could have been entirely avoided.

Besides the more obvious problems that can arise with a dog that was originally bred for hunting vermin and fighting other dogs, when not carefully raised, taught firm rules and boundaries and engaged in vigorous activities that build both body and mind, there are many possible situations or unwanted outcomes that may arise that might have been avoided.

Being aware of "mistakes" that we humans can inadvertently make can go a long way toward preventing troubles later in life. We can fall short in areas such as:

- not taking the time to properly socialise
- not desensitizing our dog to loud noises
- falling prey to those staring eyes that they know how to work to their own advantage

- feeding too much
- leaving our loyal companion alone too much
- not exercising enough
- not finding ways to mentally challenge
- accidentally rewarding our dog at the wrong time
- allowing our dog to be the boss
- not being a strong enough leader for the breed we choose
- not having the knowledge we need to properly raise a dog
- not being aware of a particular breed's special needs
- not taking the time to teach basic rules and boundaries
- not being honest about our own energy level
- not being honest about how much time we can devote to a dog

All of these and more can inadvertently create frustration and unwanted behaviours that lead to health issues that could have been entirely avoided.

As well, not being aware of the adolescent craziness time in a young dog's life and how to get through it, and many other less obvious mistakes, such as choosing the wrong collar or leash, allowing your dog to sleep in your bed, or free feeding can all result in the creation of problems.

While we humans may be well meaning, besides the obvious disasters that we can create when we don't properly train or socialise our canine friends, we can inadvertently make a lot of mistakes when raising our canine companions that will cause our fur friends to needlessly suffer.

Let's begin with the more obvious *"Preventing Socialisation Behavioural Issues"* that can lead to unsettling problems later in life, and proceed further into areas of *"Accidental Rewards"* that may not be so obvious, then touch upon *"Basic Rules and Boundaries"* and *"Adolescent Craziness"*, and finish this chapter with *"Less Obvious Human Mistakes"*.

Preventing Socialisation Behavioural Issues

In order to prevent behavioural issues, you first need to be aware of how easy it is to inadvertently create them yourself.

Much of how your chosen dog learns to behave will depend entirely upon you, how extensively they were socialised as a puppy and how much they are continually being socialised throughout their life.

Without proper socialisation, even the most naturally polite dog can become neurotic, overly bossy, nervous, unsociable, and learn to act out aggressively toward unknown dogs, smaller animals or people. This is a situation that can get any dog labelled nasty or even dangerous should they act out aggressively for any reason, and those who are aware of the Staffy's fighting history will be even less tolerant.

Many people don't realize how important it is to properly and continually socialise their dogs in several different areas.

FACT ***Without proper socialisation, many behavioural problems could become a daily occurrence.***

Never make the mistake of thinking that you only need to socialise your puppy during the first few months of their life and that they will then be fine for the rest of their life, because all dogs, including the Staffordshire Bull Terrier, require constant socialising.

As well, once they reach adolescence, a dog's personality can really begin to assert itself, and this is when, without constant and vigilant daily socialising and training, any unwanted aggressive or anti-social tendencies may begin to surface.

Generally speaking, the majority of an adult dog's habits and behavioural traits will be formed between the ages of birth and one year of age. While it is even more important to introduce puppies to a wide variety of sights, sounds, smells and situations during the most formative period in their young life, which is usually their first 16 weeks, all dogs, no matter their age or breed, need to be exposed to different people, dogs, animals, places and unusual sights and sounds throughout their entire adult life.

Socialising With Unknown Dogs

Any dog, despite their natural personality, that is not regularly socialised may become shy, nervous, afraid, suspicious or overly bossy around unfamiliar or unusual dogs, animals, people or circumstances. In the case of the confident and fearless Staffy, this can then lead to unacceptable dominance aggression.

Daily on-leash dog walks are the perfect opportunities for your dog to see and possibly meet other dogs and different people, as well as practice proper behaviour when out and about.

Remember to take it slowly and never put your fur friend in an uncomfortable situation where he or she feels forced into being around other canines they may be unsettled around. Your dog should always be given the option to walk away, with lots of space.

When socialising a young puppy, remember to introduce him or her first to the *more calm and friendlier* of dogs, because introducing your small pup to a dog that may be overly boisterous or not so friendly with other dogs may result in a negative experience that could teach your dog to take an unwanted aggressive stance.

While the Staffy is rarely ever fearful, negative experiences with other dogs at a young age may result in learning to aggressively posture when seeing unknown other dogs. I would suggest finding a local puppy class with around 8-10 other puppies, so that you can carefully supervise socialising and guided play.

Socialising With Unknown People

Proper socialisation also means taking your puppy (or dog) everywhere with you and introducing them to many different people of all ages, sizes and ethnicities, so they will learn what is normal and acceptable behaviour in their daily life.

DO NOT get into the habit of always carrying a puppy or smaller dog. They need to walk on their own feet so that they don't develop unwanted behaviour problems, such as "armpit alligator" tendencies (snapping when someone stops to say hello) that can result from being in an elevated position where they feel they are in charge and must protect <u>their</u> human.

Also important, will be getting your puppy or dog used to the unpredictable actions and often loud noise of young children. You will want to closely supervise play, so that children are not accidentally being too rough or screaming in high-pitched voices, because this can be unsettling for a young puppy or dog that is unfamiliar with children.

Be especially careful when introducing your puppy to young children who may accidentally hurt your puppy, because you don't want your dog to become fearful of children as this could lead to aggression issues later on in life. While most Terrier breeds are well known to not hesitate when it comes to protecting themselves from small children who do not understand how to respect a dog's space, this dog is usually gentle and patient. Still, you will want to keep in mind that any dog that is pushed too far may feel the need to protect his or herself from a child that is invading their space, getting too close to their toys or food bowl, or treating them roughly.

Environmental Socialisation

It can be a BIG mistake not to take the time to introduce your Staffordshire puppy to a wide variety of different environments, because when they are not comfortable with different sights, smells and sounds, this could cause them (and you) stress and trauma later in their adult life.

Be creative and take your puppy everywhere you can imagine when they are young, so that no matter where they travel, whether strolling along a crowded city sidewalk or beside a deserted shoreline, they will be equally comfortable. Also, don't forget to train this dog to calmly accept travelling inside their kennel when driving anywhere.

Do not make the mistake of only taking your puppy into areas where you live and will frequently travel, because your dog also needs to be just as comfortable visiting areas you might not often visit, such as noisy construction sites, airports or a petting zoo across town.

Your puppy needs to see all sorts of people, animals, sights, sounds and situations so that they will not become nervous or unsettled, should they need to travel with you outside of their familiar neighbourhood.

Your dog will take their cues from you, which means that when you are calm and firmly in control of every situation, they will learn to trust and calmly follow your lead.

For instance, take them to a noisy construction site, to the airport where they can watch people and hear planes landing and taking off, to a local park where they can hear a crowd and see a baseball game, for a stroll beside a schoolyard at recess time when noisy children are out playing, or to the local zoo or farm and let them get a close up look at horses, pigs, chickens and ducks. Use your imagination.

reminder

Again, never think that socialisation only takes place when your dog is a young puppy, as proper socialisation is on-going for your dog's entire life.

Fear of Loud Noises

Many dogs can show extreme fear of loud noises, such as fireworks, sirens, thunderstorms or home security alarms. We humans need to learn how to either prevent this trauma in the first place or learn how to appropriately respond to a dog that is afraid of loud noises.

When you take the time to desensitize your dog to these types of noises when they are very young, it will be much easier on them during stormy weather, holidays such as Halloween or New Year's, when fireworks are often a part of the festivities, when an ambulance or fire truck roars past with sirens wailing, or when your fire or security alarm is activated.

REMEMBER: Loud, piercing noises will be very painful for a dog's sensitive ears, so use your hands to protect their ears if you're out walking when a vehicle with a blaring siren is roaring past.

Desensitization Devices: there are several ways you can help to desensitize your dog, so that they are not traumatized by high-pitched alarms, and loud, popping or banging noises or explosions, including the following:

CDs: you can purchase CD's that are a collection of unusual sounds, such as vacuums or hoovers, airplanes, sirens, smoke alarms, fireworks, guns firing, people clapping hands, screaming children, and more (or you can easily make your own), that you can play while working in your kitchen or relaxing in your living room or lounge.

When you play these sounds and pretend that everything is normal, the next time your puppy or dog hears these types of sounds elsewhere, they will not become upset or agitated because they will have already learned to ignore them.

Bubble Wrap: is also another simple way to desensitize a dog that is fearful of unexpected popping sounds. Show them the bubble wrap, pop a few of the cells and if they do not run away, give them a treat. You can start with the bubble wrap that has small, quieter cells, and then graduate them to the larger celled (louder) bubble wrap. You can also take things even farther by blowing up some small paper bags or balloons and loudly popping them in front of your dog, or even taking them to a local rifle range.

Thunder Shirts: some dogs will respond well to wearing a *"Thunder Shirt"*, which is specifically designed to alleviate anxiety or trauma associated with loud rumbling, popping or banging noises. The idea behind the design of the Thunder Shirt is that the gentle pressure it creates is similar to a hug that, for some dogs, has a calming effect.

Relaxation Collars: there are basically two types of collars designed to help relax or calm an upset puppy or dog. One uses scent or calming pheromones, while the other uses species-specific music at appropriate decibel levels to calm a fearful or stressed dog.

TV or Radio: sometimes all that is required to calm a dog that is stressed by loud noises is to play your inside TV or Radio station with the sounds of relaxing music, louder than you might normally, to help disguise the exterior noise of fireworks or thunder.

Always be aware that some dogs literally lose their minds and do things that make no logical sense when they hear the loud popping or screeching noises of fireworks and various alarms and start trembling, running or trying to hide and you cannot communicate with them at all.

Make certain that your dog cannot harm itself trying to escape from these types of noises, and if possible, calmly hold them until they begin to relax.

For instance, my dog, Boris, used to try and escape through the drain in the bathtub (go figure), because loud popping noises literally caused him to lose his mind.

Make sure that YOU are acting appropriately yourself, by not panicking or having weak, *"feeling sorry"* or *"angry and frustrated"* energy around an upset dog, because this will only make matters worse.

When the person who is supposed to be your dog's support system is also feeling weak or acting unstable, your dog will have nowhere to turn. Instead, support them by pretending that nothing is wrong and if you must talk to them, do so in a calm, yet assertive voice.

Never underestimate the importance of taking the time to continually (not just when they are puppies) socialise and desensitize your dog to all manner of sounds. Doing so will help curb their tendency to sound off at every little noise, which will make everyone happier in the future, while teaching them to be a calm and well-balanced member of your family in every situation.

Accidental Rewards

Many times, we humans are guilty of accidentally rewarding our puppies and dogs for engaging in types of behaviour we are embarrassed about or not happy with, and the following are some of the more obvious things we may be doing that can be inadvertently rewarding, and thus encouraging, an unwanted behaviour.

Aggression Rewards

Many people unknowingly get into the habit of accidentally rewarding their puppies or dogs for displaying nervousness, fear, barking, growling or lunging at another dog or person by picking them up, talking soothingly, or offering them a treat. I see this happen all too frequently.

For instance, many people simply pick up their dog when they are acting out in an unacceptable manner. Be careful that you don't get into this bad habit.

Should you accidentally reward your dog by picking them up when they are displaying any sort of unbalanced energy, you may be silently teaching them to continue with this type of unwanted behaviour and you'll be picking them up even more.

As well, picking up a small dog or puppy when they are growling, barking or acting out inappropriately, besides being a reward, places them in much more dominant, top dog position where they literally have just gained the higher ground.

A dog in the *"top dog"* position feels more confident because they are now looking down on their target and, depending on <u>your</u> energy, will usually then become more dominant than the person or dog they may have just growled at when they were at "*ground level*".

Rather than accidentally rewarding your Staffordshire for displaying unwanted behaviour, a more effective action to take in such a situation is to keep them on the ground, and get their attention back on you. Gently correct your puppy or dog with firm yet calm energy (that is just a little stronger than the energy your dog is displaying) by distracting them with a firm

"No!" and a quick sideways snap of the leash, which should get them looking to you for direction. This will "tell" your dog that they must let you deal with whatever situation has caused them to react badly.

Should the human holding the leash allow a fearful, nervous, shy or bossy dog to deal with situations that unnerve them or cause them to bellow loudly or act out aggressively, you could be unknowingly creating a problem that has the potential to escalate into something very serious.

The same is true of situations where a young puppy may feel the need to protect itself from a larger or older dog that may come charging in for a sniff or is acting confrontational. It's much easier to prevent confrontational outbursts between dogs when the human guardian takes responsibility to protect their fur friend, so that the dog never has to feel that they must react out of fear or with aggression in order to protect his or herself or the human at the other end of the leash. Remember that the Staffy is a dog that will usually rise to any sort of challenge or aggressive stance from another dog and if you don't immediately take control, you may have a fight on your hands.

No matter the age or size of your puppy or dog, allowing them to display aggression, loud barking or any sort of unwanted behaviour toward another dog, animal or person is NEVER a laughing matter and this type of behaviour must be immediately curtailed.

Excitement Rewards

It's important to recognize that attention paid to an overly excited or out-of-control puppy or dog, even negative attention, is likely going to be rewarding for your fur friend. If your dog is feeling that he or she is not receiving enough of your attention, they are smart enough to quickly learn to do whatever it takes to get the attention they desire.

Bottom line, when you engage with an out-of-control puppy or dog, you can be actually rewarding them for acting out in an unstable manner, and inadvertently end up encouraging them to continue with more overly exuberant behaviour you might not be very pleased about.

Be careful that you're not accidentally teaching your dog to act out with crazy energy every time they see you.

For instance, chasing after a puppy when they have taken something they are not supposed to have, picking them up when they're barking or showing aggression, pushing them off when they jump on you or other people, or yelling when they refuse to come when called, can all be forms of negative attention that can be rewarding to your dog and encourage more of the same unwanted behaviour.

Instead, remain calm and consistently firm with your training, so that your dog learns how to control their energy and play appropriately without jumping on everyone or engaging in growling, barking or mouthy behaviour.

Interaction Rewards

If your Staffordshire displays excited energy simply from being petted by you, or anyone else, you will need to teach yourself, your family and your friends to ignore your fur friend until he or she calms down. Otherwise, you will be literally teaching your canine companion that the touch of humans means excitement, and this behavioural problem will continue to escalate.

For instance, when you continue to interact with an overly excited puppy or dog, you are actually rewarding them for out-of-control behaviour and essentially teaching them that when they see humans, you want them to display excited energy.

Too many people encourage their dog to be nuts, for instance, when they return home and greet their dog in a highly excited state. While it's nice to know that your dog is happy to see you, when you forget about being your dog's calm pack leader just a few times, this may be enough to send your smart dog three confusing messages: (1) that they can no longer rely upon you to be their calm leader; (2) that leadership may now be their responsibility; and (3) that seeing humans means they must display out-of-control excitement.

Instead, when you come home, greet your dog calmly and quietly, and if they are at all excited, do NOT touch or speak to them until they calm down. Otherwise, your dog will soon learn that humans are a source of excitement and confusing messages, and long, consistently vigilant work on your part (with help from your friends and family) will be the only way to reverse this chaotic behaviour.

Another thing to keep in mind is that children are often a source of high energy and excitement that can cause a puppy or dog to quickly become extremely wound up.

If you don't want to create an on-going behavioural problem, that could accidentally get someone injured, you will need to be very vigilant about NOT permitting young children to engage with an excited puppy or dog.

Important Basic Rules and Boundaries

You can prevent many future behavioural problems when you take the time to ensure that your chosen dog learns basic rules and boundaries. All that's necessary for effectively teaching your puppy (or dog) these basics is a calm, consistent and firm approach, combined with your endless patience.

Basic rules and boundaries would include things such as:

- no barking at every little noise
- no dogs allowed in the kitchen when preparing food
- no begging at the human's dinner table
- humans through the door first
- no sleeping in the human bed
- no raiding the garbage can
- no jumping up on tables or counters
- no jumping on humans
- no helping yourself to "tootsie rolls" from the cat's litter box

- no chasing the neighbour's cat
- no random digging in the flower bed

Many puppies are ready to begin basic training at about 10 to 12 weeks of age, and some will be ready at 8 weeks. However, be careful not to overdo it when they are less than four months of age, as their attention span may be short.

With younger puppies, make your training sessions no more than 5 or 10 minutes, positive and pleasant with plenty of praise and/or treats, so that your puppy will be looking forward to their next session.

Also, begin to introduce hand signals that go along with the verbal commands so that once they learn both, you can remove the verbal commands in favour of just hand signals.

When you teach a dog hand signals, they will become much more attentive because they must look at you to see what you require them to do.

Consistently teach your puppy or dog the ***All Important Three***, which are the "Come", "Sit" and "Stay" commands (more about this in Chapter 12: Training Basics For a Happy Staffordshire Bull Terrier), and use them every day in every opportunity to help your young dog progress through their unpredictable adolescent period.

Adolescent Craziness

Too often, we humans become frustrated and impatient and give up on our dogs when they transition from being the cute, cuddly and mostly obedient little puppy they once were and become all kinds of craziness.

Instead of riding the adolescent storm, it can often be during this confusing and trying adolescent stage of a dog's life that they end up behind bars when the humans who promised to love and protect them, abandon their once happy fur friend at the local SPCA or rescue facility.

With consistency, understanding, the right information, and endless patience and perseverance, you and your fur friend can emerge out the other side of this adolescent period with a much stronger bond.

Firstly, you need to know that not all dogs go through an intensely crazy adolescent period. Secondly, when you remain consistent with your socialising and training during this time, you can live through puppy adolescence and come out the other side a much more knowledgeable and patient guardian.

Remember, you've already lived through potty training, teething, socialising and basic rules and boundaries with your young dog, and you need to feel proud of all your accomplishments and the leaps and bounds you and your puppy have accomplished together over the last several months.

If your adolescent dog is now beginning to act out and push your buttons, rather than giving up on them, it's time to remain calm, consistent and persistent, and re-visit basic rules and boundaries, while keeping in mind that you will eventually be able to enjoy the happy rewards that all those months of diligent puppy training have brought to your relationship.

During adolescence, you may experience several changes in your dog's personality that you're not exactly pleased about. For instance, your young Terrier may:

- no longer be as friendly with strangers
- begin to show their aggressive side to other dogs
- start to be possessive of their human
- start to bark at unknown people and dogs
- begin to excavate the back yard
- become possessive of toys or their food bowl
- look for opportunities to chase the neighbour's cat
- start to show their stubborn side

- ignore you when called
- appear to have suddenly gone deaf
- ignore the basic commands they've already learned
- start to relieve themselves inside again
- bark or whine when left alone
- begin to mark territory
- try to escape the back yard

Welcome to the world of canine adolescence, where it appears that all your previous work has flown out the window and your puppy has turned into some sort of monster.

DON'T PANIC, because every dog is different and your dog's adolescent period may pass by without notice. However, being prepared for the worst will help you ride any impending storm and help to get you both safely out the other side where you can enjoy an even closer relationship than you previously had.

The adolescent phase may be very subtle for your puppy, or it may be so dramatic that frustration with your fur friend is becoming a daily occurrence and you're questioning whether you made the right choice to invite a dog into your life.

If frustration is getting the upper hand, rather than letting it get worse, consider the benefits of hiring a professional, who can provide insight and valuable assistance to help you through this stage of your puppy's development.

Less Obvious Human Mistakes

There are many less obvious mistakes we humans can inadvertently make with our dogs that can also lead to behavioural problems later in life, some of which include:

Sleeping in Your Bed: many people make the mistake of allowing an adorable crying puppy to sleep with them in their bed. While this may help to calm and comfort a new puppy, it will set a dangerous precedent that can result in behavioural problems later in their life. As well, a sleeping human body could easily crush a small puppy.

As much as it may pull on your heart strings to hear your new puppy crying the first couple of nights in their kennel, a little tough love at the beginning will keep them safe while helping them to learn to both love and respect you as their leader.

FACT ***Be aware that it's perfectly fine and natural for your puppy or dog to sleep in the same room with you. After all, they are part of your "pack" and need to be near. Just make sure that you don't let him or her take over YOUR bed.***

Picking Them Up at the Wrong Time: never pick your puppy up if they display nervousness, fear or aggression (such as growling) toward an object, person or other pet, because this will be rewarding them for displaying unbalanced behaviour.

Instead, your puppy needs to be gently corrected by you, with firm and calm energy, so that they learn not to react with fear or aggression.

Armpit Alligators: when your dog is a small puppy, be aware that many guardians get into the bad habit of carrying a small dog or puppy far too much.

Remember that they need to be on the ground and walking on their own, so that they do not become overly confident. A dog that is carried by their guardian is literally being placed in the *"top dog"* position.

Be aware that humans who constantly carry small dogs or puppies, rather than allowing them to walk on their own, can often inadvertently create what I refer to as an *"armpit alligator"* situation. This is where you see someone carrying a cute little dog and you stop to say hello, only to be greeted by snapping jaws and sharp teeth.

Even dogs that are usually polite and not naturally wary or suspicious of strangers can learn to become intolerant if they don't receive adequate socialisation. The Staffordshire may already have a naturally dominant personality, which means that if their human guardians are not in control, this dog may soon become protective or possessive of *"their"* humans.

Playing Too Hard or Too Long: many humans play too hard or allow their children to play too long or too roughly with their puppy. You need to remember that your young puppy tires very easily and especially during the critical growing phases of their young life, they need their rest.

Hand Play: always discourage your puppy from chewing or biting your hands, or any part of your body for that matter.

Do NOT get into the habit of playing the *"hand"* game, where you rough up your puppy and slide them across the floor with your hands, because this will teach them that your hands are playthings and you will have to work long and hard to break this bad habit.

PERSONAL EXPERIENCE: When my puppy came home with me at 10-weeks of age, the breeder had already been playing the hand game and it took me a very long time to teach my Boris that biting human hands was not acceptable behaviour. Interestingly, when he sees people that he has not seen for years, that he used to know when he was a young puppy, this old habit often re-surfaces for a short while.

When your puppy is teething, they will naturally want to chew on everything within reach, and this will include you. As cute as you might think it is, this is not an acceptable behaviour and you need to gently, but firmly, discourage the habit.

A light flick with a finger on the end of your puppy's nose, combined with a firm "NO" and removing the enticing fingers by making a fist when they are trying to bite those human fingers, plus giving them a toy that they CAN chew, will quickly discourage them from this activity.

Not Getting Used to Grooming: not taking the time to get your dog used to a regular grooming routine, including bathing, brushing, toenail clipping and teeth brushing, can lead to a lifetime of trauma for both human and dog every time these procedures must be performed.

reminder

Set aside several minutes each day or two for your grooming routine.

NOTE: get your puppy used to being up high on a table or countertop when it's grooming time. This way, when they visit the vet's office, where they will be placed on an examination table, they will not be stressed because this will already be a familiar situation.

Free Feeding: means to keep food in your puppy's bowl 24/7, so that they can eat any time of the day or night, whenever they feel like it.

While free feeding a young puppy can be a good idea (especially with very small dogs), until they are about four or five months old, many guardians often get into the bad habit of allowing their adult dogs to continue to eat food any time they want, by leaving food out 24/7.

The Staffordshire Bull Terrier is usually quite food motivated, which means if there is food out, they will probably eat it. However, while every dog is different, you don't want to get into the habit of leaving food out 24/7 because (a) they no longer associate you being in control of the food, and (b) if your particular dog gets used to eating too much, they will quickly gain weight and become obese, which can lead to health issues that may shorten their life.

Getting into a free feeding habit can be a serious mistake, as your dog is not a cat, and needs to know that you are absolutely in control of their food. Food is a very powerful motivator for dogs, and you being clearly in control of the food will help to establish you as a powerful leader in your dog's mind.

Treating Them Like Children: do not get into the bad habit of treating your dog like a small, furry human; even though they may try their best to please you and their doggy smarts could help them to succeed in most instances, not honouring them for being an amazing dog will only cause them confusion that could lead to future behavioural problems.

reminder

Remember that the one thing your dog is the absolute BEST at, is Being a Dog.

A well-balanced dog thrives on rules and boundaries, and when they have a consistently strong human leader, they can relax because they will understand that there is no question that you are their leader and they are your follower. This means that they will not be faced with having to make human decisions, and can live a contented, stress-free life.

Distraction and Replacement: when your puppy tries to chew on your hand, foot, clothing, or anything else that is not fair game, you need to firmly and calmly tell them "NO", and then distract them by replacing what they are not supposed to be chewing with something they are permitted to chew, such as an appropriate toy.

Make sure that you happily praise your puppy every time they choose the toy to chew on. If they persist in chewing on you, remove yourself from the equation by getting up and walking away. If they are really persistent, put them inside their kennel with a favourite chew toy until they calm down.

Always praise your puppy when they stop inappropriate behaviour or replace inappropriate behaviour with something that is acceptable to you, so that they begin to understand what they can and cannot do.

Flat Collar Nightmares

Many humans simply don't realize how important it is to choose the "right" kind of collar for their canine companion. Add this to the fact that there is an ever-increasing array of tempting colours and styles to choose from and it's very easy to get distracted and forget about choosing what is most appropriate for your dog.

What you really need in a collar is one that will also keep your dog safe and secure. While the flat collar may be fine for a calm dog that never pulls, leaps about or suddenly tries to do an about face and take off running in a different direction to chase that teasing squirrel or taunting cat, this is not a very safe reality.

After 40 some years of working with dogs and experiencing possibly every type of terrifying, unexpected disaster while out walking a dog, the ONLY collar I feel absolutely confident using (because I know that the dog I'm in control of cannot wiggle out of it), is the "Martingale" collar.

Flat collars, unless you have them cinched up so tight that you're almost cutting off your dog's air supply, can be fairly easy for most dogs to get out of.

All dogs are amazing athletes, and even though you may have a firm grip on that leash, they can back away from you, wiggle, twist and contort themselves in a quick instant, flip their head and the collar is off – bye, bye doggy!

The Martingale Collar

There are several reasons why the Martingale dog collar **(see photo below)** is far superior to a flat collar:

- comfortable for your dog to wear all day long
- safe because your dog cannot wiggle out of it
- best training collar

The Martingale collar looks much the same as a flat collar, with one very important difference – there is a triangular piece of chain in the middle of it. This chain is attached to the collar with two rings, with a third ring in the middle of the chain, which is where you attach your leash.

When there is no tension on the collar (from them pulling on the leash), the collar hangs loose and comfortable. However, when there IS tension on the collar, that little piece of chain tightens so that your dog cannot get out of their collar.

PERSONAL EXPERIENCE: My dog Boris, despite his short nose, wore the same Martingale "training" collar for almost 15 years. This collar conveys important messages between dog and human.

That little piece of triangular chain makes a slight noise when you sharply tug or jiggle it, and this sends a message to your dog that you want their attention on you. It's simply the best collar for teaching your dog to walk calmly by your side and to remind them that YOU are in charge.

When buying a Martingale collar for your Staffy, take him or her with you because it needs to be the correct size to fit over the widest part of their head. Then, once you've got the right size for your dog, you need to pay strict attention to the correct way to adjust the collar for maximum effect and safety.

Adjusting the Martingale Collar: once you've placed the collar over your dog's head, it's important that you properly adjust it. You need to adjust the length so that when you attach the leash to the outside ring and pull it tight, when the two inside rings come together there is still a gap between these two rings of approximately two human finger widths. You never want the two inside rings to touch.

You can now enjoy comfortable and safe walks with your happy companion.

Flexi-Leash Fiasco

Personally, flexi, retractable or extendable dog leashes **(see photo below)** are high on my list of pet peeves for several important reasons, including that they:

- are dangerous for human and dog alike
- allow the dog to be in the wrong walking position
- allow the humans to forget their responsibilities
- are heavy, clumsy and difficult to securely grip
- are an excuse for not properly training your dog

- can accidentally break
- can cause fights between dogs

While many people believe that a retractable leash is a good way to allow their dogs more freedom to roam while still keeping them securely attached, the above reasons highlight why these leashes can be a very bad idea. See below for more details.

Injury to human and dog: these leashes are usually spring-loaded, many feet long (usually 26 feet or 7.9 meters), and thin cords wound up inside a cumbersome plastic compartment with a handle and a button to control how much of the leash is extended.

As you can imagine, it's far more difficult to control a dog that is roaming about 20 or more feet away from you, than it would be if they were attached to a standard 4 to 6 foot leash and walking at your side.

If your dog gets used to having a 20-foot (6 meter) or more leeway, they will soon forget about you, be busy sniffing interesting scents, and can quickly run out into traffic. They can be surprised by another dog rushing in, or get tangled up with a person and a dog, which can cause both injury to the dogs and people, or may cause a fight between the two dogs.

These leashes are also serious tripping hazards that can cause many injuries.

MEMORY LANE: The daughter of one of my dog whispering clients broke her toe as a result of tripping over a flexi-leash, I have suffered painful "rope" burns several times, and once was hit in the head (ouch!) with the hard and heavy plastic handle as it snapped back when the person holding it lost their grip and dropped it.

In addition, every flexi or retractable leash is equipped with a brake to stop the unwinding of the cord at various lengths. If your dog is running and all of a sudden comes to the end of their freedom, unless you drop the handle, they will be forced to come to a very abrupt stop that can injure a dog's neck or spine.

Incorrect Walking Position: the ONLY place your dog should ever be when you're out walking is beside you, and when you allow them to freely roam 20 or more feet from wherever you are, besides being lax about teaching your dog the correct walking position, you are *"telling"* them that you are no longer in charge. A dog that believes they are in charge can get you BOTH into a lot of trouble.

Forgetting Your Human Responsibilities: when you're out walking with your puppy or dog, as their leader, you are responsible for everything they do, including picking up after them. A retractable leash allows your dog to literally be out of your sight. While you're busy chatting with a neighbour or checking your phone messages, you may not be aware of what sort of *"message"* your dog may be depositing in the neighbour's yard.

You can be fined for not picking up after your dog, not to mention gaining yourself a bad reputation from your neighbours or other more responsible dog walkers.

Difficult to Securely Grip: the flexi leash has a large, cumbersome handle that is quite slippery and difficult to securely hold onto. If your companion suddenly lunges or changes direction, the chances of you losing your grip are quite high, and when that happens, the consequences can be dangerously grave.

Once dropped, your dog is now dragging a bouncing, loudly clattering handle, which can be very noisy on a sidewalk or hard surface.

MEMORY LANE: This very thing has happened to me in a busy, high traffic area, when walking someone else's dog. While I was lucky and managed to get him safely back, I can tell you from first-hand experience that this is a highly stressful and frightening situation I would not want to wish on anyone.

Unless your dog has been trained to remain calmly sitting at your side while rifles are fired near their head, this loudly clattering flexi leash that seems to be chasing them can be a very scary experience that will cause most dogs to run.

When your dog is scared, they will run even faster, while you run after them adding to the chaos with your panic-stricken screams to stop before they get killed trying to cross a busy intersection. Not a good scene.

Poor Training: while many might believe they are giving their dog more freedom by using a retractable leash, they are actually missing out on properly training their dog to heel beside them and to respond appropriately to the all-important "come" or "recall" command.

The very nature of a flexi leash is such that the dog is often out in front of the person who is supposed to be in charge, and always *"pulling"*, which to an approaching dog can look like an aggressive stance, resulting in the other dog thinking he or she must retaliate with a defensive stance. All of this, as you can imagine, has the potential to result in a scuffle between dogs and humans.

Accidental Breakage: there is a great deal of wear on a small diameter cord that is constantly unwinding and rewinding and you may not notice a worn area until it actually breaks. Then, you've got a potential runaway dog disaster to hopefully recover from, before the dog gets severely injured, killed by a vehicle, or ends up in some other type of serious trouble.

Improve your training, have better control, make your life easier, avoid injuries, and ensure the safety and security of yourself and your furry best friend by choosing a Martingale collar and a standard 4-foot leash.

Sled Dog Fiasco

One last thought about what I call the *"Sled Dog Fiasco"*. Many people think that buying a harness is a better choice than the proper collar for their canine companion.

However, the only time a harness is actually the right choice is if you have a Springer for your bicycle, or a strong sled dog that you need to put in harness, so that they can pull you.

While a harness may be helpful in some circumstances, as a regular walking arrangement, there are reasons why this may not be the best choice.

What happens when you put most dogs in a harness is that (1) they are automatically in the wrong walking position, being head and shoulders in front of you; (2) you no longer have control of their head and cannot correct unwanted behaviour; and (3) they now are in control of you and are much more powerful and potentially difficult to control, because the entire weight and strength of their body is attached to that harness.

Take Away Tip: "Harnesses are for sled dogs".

In a Nutshell

It cannot be emphasized strongly enough how important it is to properly socialise your puppy, and understand that we humans often unknowingly reward our dogs at the wrong time, which can actually cause behavioural issues later in life.

Re-visit this Chapter information and think about what other mistakes you may be inadvertently making, so that you can do your best to avoid simple mistakes we humans often are guilty of making with our dogs, that can lead to an unhappy dog that suffers from behavioural problems later in life.

Also, when training your dog, keep in mind that the type of leash and collar you choose can make a big difference.

Chapter 11: Happy Staffordshire Bull Terrier Body Language

"Money can buy a fine dog, but
only love can make him wag his tail."
— Kinky Friedman

We all know good communication is not just about the words we use. Our tone of voice, energy and our body language help to package up and deliver our meaning every day.

While most people can effectively communicate their thoughts and feelings through words, we need to generally be reliant upon reading our dog's body language in order to know if they are happy, sad, nervous, afraid or aggressive.

Because our dogs don't speak our language, the only way to truly comprehend and effectively communicate with them is for us to understand and appreciate what they are telling us through their body and the vocal sounds they make.

Often, gestures or actions that we assume mean one thing are actually the dog telling us the exact opposite, and determining what that wagging tail or barking really means can sometimes be the difference between a belly rub and a bite.

How happy would you be if you could not communicate with your family at home? Would you develop behaviour issues over time? Of course, you would, and the same is also true for your beloved dog.

They need you to understand what they are *"telling you"* and how they feel, in order to be a happy family member. For instance, learning to properly "read" your dog's intentions can easily prevent an unwanted encounter during a visit to the local dog park.

Therefore, taking the time to educate yourself about basic canine body language and paying attention to your dog's particular body language (including their face, posture, barking and tail position) is an important prerequisite for raising a content and well-behaved dog.

This Chapter will teach you exactly that – to understand the basics of what your furry friend (and those dogs around you) are trying to *"tell"* you and how they feel, so that you can share a happy lifelong partnership together.

So, don't wait because now is a good time to start developing and honing your canine body language skills.

What's With All the Wagging and Barking?

While a well-socialised Staffordshire Bull Terrier may often happily wag their tail, it can be a mistake to automatically assume that if your dog, or someone else's dog is wagging their tail, that they are happy and friendly.

What Does the Wag Mean?

When determining a dog's true intent or demeanour, it's important to take into consideration the complete dog posture, rather than just the tail, because it's entirely possible that a dog can be wagging his or her tail just before it decides to take an aggressive lunge toward you or your dog.

More important in determining the emotional state of most dogs is the height or positioning of their tail. For instance, a tail that is held parallel to your dog's back usually suggests that they are feeling relaxed, whereas if the tail is held stiffly vertical, this usually means that they may be feeling aggressive or dominant.

Also keep in mind that certain dog tails are carried differently for different reasons. Depending on which dog tail, you will have more or less visible cues. The opposite is also true of other dogs reading your dog's body language.

For instance, a dog with a docked or tightly curled tail can sometimes send confusing messages to others.

A tail held much lower can mean that your dog is feeling stressed, afraid, submissive or unwell and if the tail is tucked underneath the dog's body, this is most often a sign that the dog is feeling highly stressed, nervous, fearful or threatened by another dog, person or unfamiliar situation.

Paying attention to your dog's tail (and any dog tails around you) can help you to know when you need to step in and make some space between your dog and another, more dominant or nervous dog.

Of course, different breeds naturally carry their tails at different heights, and some dogs have tightly curled, short or docked tails, while others may not have any visible tail at all. You will need to take this into consideration so that you get used to their particular body language signals.

As well, the speed at which the tail is moving will give you an idea of the mental state of your dog, because the speed of the wag usually indicates how excited a dog may be.

For instance, a slow, slightly swinging wag can often mean that a dog is tentative about greeting another dog, and this is more of a questioning type of wag, whereas a fast-moving tail held high can mean that your dog is about to challenge or threaten another less dominant dog.

Also, a stalking stance, where a dog has raised hackles (hair along the back), lowers their head, crouches and slowly creeps forward with an intense stare often happens just before a serious attack. There is also a similar-looking *"play"* stance, and without practice, you may have difficulty identifying the difference between the two.

MEMORY LANE: I've been sworn at after politely letting a guardian of a larger dog, who was unaware (and didn't want to know) that their dog was stalking my smaller dog and about to do him harm, so be careful how you approach these situations.

What Does the Bark Mean?

Of course, our dogs bark for a wide variety of reasons, and every dog is different, depending upon their natural breed tendencies and how they were raised. In the case of the Staffordshire, barking may occur when bored and stressed from being left alone or in excited anticipation of a walk or a game of fetch. This section discusses some of the more common reasons why a dog might be barking.

Communication: since the very first dog, they have communicated over long distances by howling to one another and when in closer proximity, barking to warn off other dogs approaching what they consider to be their territory, or in excitement or happiness when greeting another returning member of the dog pack.

Now, our domesticated dogs have learned to bark for a wide variety of reasons, such as when they sense danger or are alerting us to someone approaching the home.

A dog will also bark in anticipation of their favourite food, when they are afraid, frustrated, bored, excited, or to let us know they want to play. Barking is an effective way to get the attention of us humans because barking is a loud and difficult noise to ignore.

Danger: many dogs will bark to alert us to visitors or intruders, and we need to learn how to understand the difference between what our dogs perceive as danger and what is truly dangerous, or indeed how to teach our best friends the difference.

We want our dogs to tell us when there is real, imminent danger and in this case, should the danger involve an unwanted intruder, we want them to bark loudly to possibly scare this threat away.

When our dogs are barking for a reason we are not yet aware of, we need to calmly assess the situation rather than immediately becoming annoyed.

We also need to remember that a dog's sense of smell, hearing and sometimes eyesight is far more acute than our own, which means that we need to give them an opportunity to tell us if they just heard, saw or sensed something that they are worried or uncertain about. While any dog can learn to be a big barker, all dogs are unique, and much depends on how they were raised. If your dog seems to be overly eager to bark at everything, you will need to take the time to teach him or her when to stop.

Rather than ignoring our dogs (or yelling at them) when they are attempting to *"tell"* us that something is bothering them, even if we ourselves understand that the noise the dog just heard is only the neighbour's kids coming home from school or a postal delivery, we need to respond appropriately.

We need to calmly acknowledge our dog's concern by saying, *"OK, good dog,"* and then ask them to come to you. This way you have quietly and calmly let your dog know that the situation is nothing to be concerned about and you have asked them to move away from the target they are concerned about, which places you in control, and which will usually stop the barking.

Attention: many dogs will learn to bark to get their owner's attention, just because they are bored or want to be taken outside for an interesting walk or a trip to the local park to chase a ball.

Our canine companions are very good at manipulating us in this way, and if we fall for it, we can be setting ourselves up an annoying precedent that could plague us for the remainder of our relationship.

MEMORY LANE: *I shared my life with a Blue Heeler who would go berserk with loud barking every time we drove near a park or when we arrived at a park. Even so, I would never reward him for barking, because as annoying and hard on the eardrums as it was, I had to sit calmly inside the vehicle until he stopped barking. If I had let him immediately bound out of the vehicle, I would have inadvertently taught my dog that barking got him exactly what he wanted.*

When a dog is barking to gain their guardian's attention, for whatever reason, before we immediately capitulate, first we need to calmly ask our dog to make eye contact with us, and do something we ask of them. After our dog has performed a calm and quiet task for us, such as sit or lie down, then we can decide to give our dog our undivided attention on our terms.

TIP ***If you are having difficulties teaching your dog to cease and desist from too much barking, often teaching them to bark on command (with a hand signal) will solve the problem. Once a dog learns to bark with a hand signal, they will often stop the random barking, because they will be waiting for you to ask them to bark.***

Often you will see a dog and their guardian at the local dog park playing fetch and when the human is not throwing that ball quickly enough to satisfy the dog's desire to run and fetch, the dog will be madly barking at the guardian. This is the equivalent of being sworn at in doggy language.

Be careful that you're not making the mistake of allowing your puppy or dog to manipulate you in this type of situation, because if you do, you will soon create a bad habit that will very quickly become not just annoying to you, but also irritating to everyone else at the park.

Before throwing a ball or Frisbee for a dog that loves to chase and retrieve (like the Staffy), it's important to always ask the dog to sit and make eye contact with you.

Often the types of canines that are overly exuberant with chasing a ball or Frisbee have usually learned this barking behaviour from their humans, who allowed themselves to be literally at the beck and call of their dog, and created this noisy habit by throwing the ball every time the dog barked.

In this situation, if you allow your dog to dictate to you when you will throw the ball, it will take no time at all for them to learn that barking gets them their desired result, and you may have just created an annoying, rude dog who is yelling at you in doggy language to do their bidding.

In this type of ball-retrieving scenario, the dog has become ball *"obsessed"* and is no longer really paying attention to the guardian's commands, because they are solely focusing on where the ball is.

While there are many situations in which your dog may bark to convey that they've heard a noise, in all other situations where the barking is demanding an action, attention, a toy, other object or food, this is when you need to ask them to do something for you, and then only if you want to give them what they are asking for, do you follow through.

MEMORY LANE: I once had a client whose dog would start to loudly bark and howl every time he answered the phone. As you can imagine, this was big time annoying because nobody could hear what was being said. After a quick dog whispering session, this noisy canine companion quickly learned that this was not acceptable behaviour and the problem was solved.

Bottom line, remember to stay calm when your cute puppy is demanding attention, because even negative attention can be rewarding for your dog, and can lead down a future, unwanted path where he or she will learn further habits that will not be particularly endearing for the human side of the relationship once the cute puppy has become an adult.

Boredom or Separation Anxiety: many dogs, especially those who have not been properly trained, are treated like children, are under-exercised, or that have not been allowed to understand that they have rules and boundaries, will sharply bark when left at home and are bored or are feeling the anxiety of being separated from their humans.

reminder ***Many times, we humans believe that our dog is barking when being left alone, because he or she is experiencing "separation anxiety", when in fact what the dog is really experiencing is the frustration of observing a member of the pack which they believe to be their follower (i.e., You) leaving them.***

This can happen when you are not a strong enough leader for your smart, fearless Terrier and he or she has taken over. They may then loudly verbalize their frustration and displeasure because, in the dog world, the pack follower (which you may have allowed yourself to become) does NOT leave the pack leader (them). *I've seen this type of situation many times over, and once the human side of the relationship steps up and takes control, it quickly reverses.*

Breaking your dog of the habit of loud barking when they are left alone can be solved in different ways, with the most obvious being that you simply take your dog with you wherever you go. After all, they are pack animals, and in order for them to be really happy and well balanced, they need the constant direction of their leader (which is supposed to be you).

Another much more time-consuming way to solve a barking problem, could involve hiring a professional to help assess why the problem has occurred in the first place and then devise an effective plan to reverse the problem that will work for each unique situation.

Fear or Pain: another reason your dog may bark is when they are very frightened or in pain and this is usually a type of bark that sounds quite different from all the others, often being a combination of a bark and a whine, or a yelping type of noise.

This is a bark that you will want to pay close attention to, so that you can quickly respond and offer the assistance that your puppy or dog may need.

Whatever the reason your dog may be barking for, always remember that this is how they communicate and *"tell"* us that they want something or are concerned, afraid, nervous or unhappy about something, and as their guardians, we humans need to pay attention.

Raised Hackles: when your dog approaches with raised hackles (the hair along the dog's back), while this can be an indication that the dog may be approaching with dominant or aggressive tendencies, it also may be an indication that he or she is excited, fearful, startled, anxious or lacks confidence.

In any of these circumstances (whether it's your dog or someone else's), it's a good idea to be respectful and keep your distance until you can assess what's really going on. A dog that is being nervous, anxious or fearful can quickly turn into a reactive biting dog, and I can tell you from personal experience that being bitten by any dog really hurts.

The Staffy Face: dogs like the Staffordshire Bull Terrier, and other similar looking breeds have a very wide, smiling mouth that is often open widely during exercise and because it is quite different looking can send the wrong message. Be aware that this wide facial expression can cause another dog to think that your dog is approaching with an aggressive stance.

<u>In a Nutshell</u>

Learning your dog's particular body language can take some time, and this Chapter will help you get started. The more you are out and about with your dog, visiting and socialising in local parks and going on walks where you will find other dogs, animals and people to observe, the more opportunity you will have to become skilled at recognizing the many subtleties of canine body language.

Paying attention to your dog's verbal and body-language signals as explained above, will help you figure out what message they are trying to get across to you and this can make all the difference in preventing frustration and unwanted encounters for you both while raising a happy and well-behaved dog.

One last thought about body language and energy – check in with your own body language and energy before you walk out the door attached to your dog. This can be more important than you might imagine, because if you're not in the moment and have your mind on something that has nothing to do with having a successful and pleasant walk with your dog, you may be setting yourself up for trouble.

For example, if you go out the door with your dog while displaying sad, weak, fearful, distracted or confusing energy, your dog will pick up on this and become nervous or confused and wonder if leadership has just defaulted to them. In other words, if your energy is not clearly conveying to your dog that you are in charge, you can literally be the cause of an uncomfortable or aggressive encounter with another person walking their dog.

It's VERY important to keep in mind that when walking with a dog (especially a strong and fearless one), the moment he or she senses that you are no longer completely in control, they will take this unspoken "cue" from you that being in charge has now defaulted to them.

You never want any dog to feel they must protect you from the postman, neighbour's cat or that taunting little Chihuahua walking across the street, because if they do, you're literally out walking with a highly charged, unpredictable, live "weapon" that could decide to go off at any moment.

Most Staffordshire Bull Terrier s will be polite when out walking, IF you are in charge and IF you have put in the time to properly train and socialise them, but they will also be imposing and fearless and will not back down if they feel challenged by another dog.

Never forget that this tenacious breed was originally a strong, working dog that would exterminate rats and fight other dogs. Therefore, should you permit your dog to take their prey drive into their own paws and, for instance, terrorize the neighbour's cat, you could end up with a lawsuit on your hands, and/or sky-high veterinary bills if this companion is permitted to be confrontational with another animal, and that's if you're lucky.

While it would usually be a rare occurrence for the Staffordshire to harm a human, the same may not hold true when encountering an unknown dog that approaches with an aggressive or challenging stance.

It's always a good idea to keep in mind that if your dog harms another dog, animal or person, or causes stress should your dog try to chase, the consequences could be far worse than a high vet bill. For instance, any dog that bites could face a death sentence or a ruling that they can never be seen in public unless they're wearing a muzzle.

Chapter 12: Training Basics for a Happy Staffordshire Bull Terrier

"Everyone thinks they have the best dog in the world. None of them are wrong."
— Unknown

It's no surprise that a properly trained dog will be a much happier, safe and more secure companion that everyone enjoys being around, and that will be far less likely to develop behaviour issues later in life.

When your dog respects your leadership and there is no question that YOU are in charge, your dog can then relax and let you take the lead on training them, which is as it should be.

Developing a basic training program and learning to teach the bright and athletic Staffordshire commands and discipline is all part of establishing yourself as the leader and starting your dog off on the right paw.

Therefore, this Chapter will focus on training basics and tips, including hand signals, as well as simple tricks that your dog will love to learn. Take heed humans, because you will be very glad that you spent the time to learn everything contained in these pages.

All of our canine companions are amazing, natural athletes and because of this, no matter their size or breed, they need humans to lead them and daily mental and physical exercise to keep them fit and healthy, so that they can be happy and well-mannered family members. Part of every dog's exercise routine includes learning at least three very important training basics, which are **"Come – Sit – Stay".**

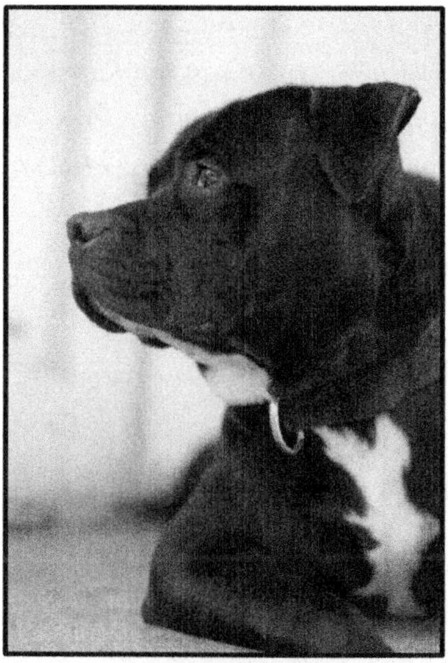

This strong and muscular dog is an athletic companion that needs vigorous daily activity to prevent them from becoming overweight and unsettled. He or she will love going for hikes, jogging, brisk walks and endless adventures with you. Most of all, these dogs will live for as much vigorous outdoor activity as possible with their guardian, and when well socialised, may also enjoy playing with other known dogs.

A happy and contented Staffy needs disciplined exercise every day to prevent the anxiety and frustration that can build up until it has nowhere to go except to display itself through barking and destructive behaviour.

If you find that your dog is being a pest by chewing inappropriate items around the home, being demanding of your time, or especially unruly when visitors come to call, this is likely because their mind is not being challenged enough or their body is not being exercised often enough, vigorously enough, or long enough each day to drain out their daily pent-up energy reserves.

A healthy, adult dog will thrive when being walked several times each day and mentally challenged by being engaged in other forms of disciplined canine activity, such as Agility, Flyball, Trick Training, Barn Hunt or even Advanced Obedience.

This is a smart dog so use your imagination and find out what canine sports YOUR dog may enjoy learning. So long as you prove to him or her that you mean what you say through firm, fair direction and consistency, rather than too many treats, they will not feel the need to manipulate or question your authority, and will happily follow your direction.

Even at the young age of eight to ten weeks, most dogs are capable of beginning to learn anything you can teach. If you wait until this strong dog is six months old before beginning any serious training program, you could already have a determined and stubborn problem on your hands and a wilful dog that may be unwilling to heed your commands.

FACT ***The backbone of helping to develop a well-balanced and happy dog is to provide them with a routine that ensures sufficient time to satisfy their particular daily physical and mental exercise needs; that might include a canine sport, plus ensuring they can be with you for almost all of their time, in combination with the opportunity to play, freely run, sniff, search and explore their world every day.***

What you can teach this active and agile canine companion depends entirely upon you and the time and patience you have to devote to their education. Never under-estimate what incredible hidden talents your dog may have.

No matter what you decide to teach, always train with firm patience, kindness, consistency and positive rewards.

TIP ***Do not train with anger or raised voices as this dog wants to please and will quickly learn whatever you have the patience to teach.***

When all training sessions are happy and fun-filled with plenty of food rewards and positive reinforcement, this will ensure that your dog is a happy, attentive student who trusts and respects you as their leader and looks forward to learning new commands, tricks and routines.

<u>Staffordshire Bull Terrier Puppy Training Basics</u>

First, choose a *"Discipline Sound"* that will be the same for every human family member. This will make it much easier for your puppy to learn what they can or cannot do and will be very useful when warning or redirecting your puppy before they engage in unwanted behaviour.

The best types of sounds are short and sharp, so that you and your family members can quickly say them and so that the sound will immediately get the attention of your puppy, as you want to be able to easily interrupt or redirect them before they make a mistake.

It doesn't really matter what the sound is, so long as it gets your dog's attention and everyone in the family is consistent. A sound that is very effective in most cases is a simple *"UH!"* sound that is said sharply and with emphasis.

Most puppies and dogs respond immediately to this sound and if caught in the middle of doing something they are not supposed to be doing, they will quickly stop and give you their attention or back away from what they were doing.

Next, your puppy needs to learn the Three Most Important Words, which are ***"Come"*, *"Sit"* and *"Stay"*.** These three basic commands will ensure that your puppy remains safe in almost every circumstance.

For instance, when your puppy correctly learns the "*Come*" command, you can always quickly bring them back to you if you should see danger approaching. Also, when you teach your puppy the "*Sit*" and "*Stay*" commands, you will be further establishing your leadership role, and a puppy that understands that their human guardian is their leader will be a safe and happy follower.

Most puppies are ready to begin training at approximately 10 to 12 weeks of age (and some even earlier). When they are still very young make your training sessions no more than 5 or 10 minutes (2 or 3 times a day). Also make sure that all training sessions are positive and pleasant with lots of praise and/or treats so that your puppy will be looking forward to their next session.

To help you understand the big three commands, yours truly demonstrates what the hand signals look like in the following pictures!

COME:

The first and most important command you need to teach your puppy is the recall, or *"Come"* command.

- Begin the *"Come"* command inside your home.
- Go into a larger room, such as your living room area.
- Place your puppy in front of you and attach their leash or a longer line to their Martingale collar, while you back away from them a few feet.
- Say the command *"Come"* in an excited, happy voice and hold your arms open wide.
- If they do not immediately come to you, gently give a tug on the leash, so that they understand that they are supposed to move toward you.
- When they come to you, happily praise them and give a treat they really enjoy.

Once your puppy can accomplish a *"Come"* command almost every time inside your home, you can then graduate them to a nearby park or quiet outside area where you will repeat the process and where there will be many more distractions.

In order to keep yourself and your dog safe, he or she needs to always come to you when asked, despite whatever distractions may be nearby.

You may want to purchase an extra-long, lightweight line (25 or 50 feet), so that you are always attached to your puppy and can encourage them in the right direction should they become distracted by noises, scents and other dogs.

Try to choose a time of day when there will be fewer distractions while you are training, and remember that swiftly moving objects, dogs or other small creatures may also be a difficult distraction for a Terrier with a strong prey drive to ignore.

Once your dog always comes running when called, you will no longer need to say the "Come" word, but just show them the signal, which they will be able to see from across the park.

Keep in mind that even after teaching your Staffordshire the *"Come"* command, their nose may take precedence over the commands you are teaching when outdoors if an interesting scent or fast-moving object or creature distracts them.

Always keep a young dog on leash when working in an area where they can easily run off in pursuit of any distraction.

SIT:

The "*Sit*" and "*Stay*" commands are both easy commands to teach that will help to keep your puppy safe and out of danger in almost every circumstance. Find a quiet time to teach these commands when your puppy is not overly tired.

- Ask your puppy to "Sit" and if they do not yet understand the command, show them what you mean by gently squeezing with your thumb and middle finger the area across the back that joins with their back legs.

- Do NOT just push them down into a sit, as this can cause damage to their back or joints.
- When they sit, give them a treat and praise them.
- When you say the word "Sit", at the same time show them the hand signal for this command.
- While you can use any hand signal, the universal hand signal for "Sit" is right arm (palm open facing upward) parallel to the floor, and then raising your arm while bending at the elbow toward your right shoulder.
- Once your dog is sitting reliably for you, remove the verbal "Sit" and replace it with the hand signal.

Every time you take your dog out for a walk, which is often a cause of excitement, get into the habit of asking them to sit quietly and patiently at every stage of your walk.

For instance, ask your dog to sit and patiently wait while you put on their leash, while you put on your shoes or jacket, after you approach the door, after you are on the other side of the door, while you lock the door, every time you arrive at a street intersection or crosswalk, every time you stop during your walk to speak to a neighbour, greet a friend or admire the view, etc., and do this all in reverse when heading back home.

When you persist with the *"Sit"* training, it will soon become automatic for your dog to calmly sit every time you stop walking. ***That's called an "automatic" sit.***

When you ask your dog to sit for you, they are learning several things all at once; that they must remain calm while paying attention to you, that you are the boss, that they must look to you for direction and that they must respect you as their leader.

Keep in mind that a sitting puppy is much easier to control than one standing at the alert, ready to bolt out the door or jump on someone. As well, because the action of sitting helps to calm the mind of an excited puppy (or dog), teaching your puppy the *"Sit"* command is a very important part of their daily interactions with your family members as well as people you may meet when out on a walk.

When you ask your puppy to *"Sit"* before you interact in any way with them, before you go out, before you feed them, etc., you are helping to quiet their mind, while teaching them to look to you for direction, and at the same time making it more difficult for them to jump, lunge or disappear out a door.

STAY:

- Once your puppy can reliably "Sit", say the word "Stay" (with authority in your voice) and hold your outstretched arm, palm open toward their head while backing away a few steps.
- If they try to follow, calmly say "No" and put them back into "Sit".
- Give a treat and then say again, "Stay" with the hand signal and back away a few steps.

- Practice these three basic "Come", "Sit", "Stay" commands everywhere you go, and use the "Sit" command as much as you can to ensure its success rate.

As your puppy matures, and their attention span increases, you will be able to train for longer periods of time and introduce more complicated routines. This is a smart, alert, thinking dog that can easily learn many hand signals.

Hand Signals

It's really important to use the hand signals that go along with the verbal commands during training, so that once your furry student learns both, you can remove the verbal commands in favour of just hand signals.

As well as being a more natural way for your dog to communicate, hand signal training is by far the most useful and efficient training method for your dog. All too often we inundate our canine companions with a great deal of chatter and noise that they really don't understand, but because they are so willing to be part of our world, they soon learn the meaning of many words.

Contrary to what some people might think, the first language of every dog is a combination of sensing energy and watching body language, which requires no spoken word or sound.

Therefore, when we humans take the time to teach our dog hand signals for all their basic commands, we are communicating with them at a level they instinctively understand, plus we are helping them to become a focused follower, as they must watch us in order to understand what is required of them.

Simple Tricks

When teaching your dog tricks, in order to give him or her extra incentive, find a treat that they really like and give the treat as a positive reward, which will help solidify a good performance.

Most dogs will be extra attentive during training sessions when they know that they will be rewarded with their favourite treats – especially this dog, who will usually have a healthy appetite.

If your puppy is less than six months old when you begin teaching them tricks, keep your training sessions short (no more than 5 or 10 minutes) and always fun. As they become adults, you can extend your sessions, as they will be able to maintain their focus for longer periods of time.

SHAKE A PAW:

Who doesn't love a well-trained dog that knows how to shake a paw? This is one of the easiest tricks to teach your dog.

- Find a quiet place to practice, without noisy distractions or other pets, and stand or sit in front of your dog.
- Place them in the sitting position and have a treat in your left hand.
- Say the command "Shake" while putting your right hand behind their left or right paw and pulling the paw gently toward yourself until you are holding their paw in your hand.
- Immediately praise them and give them their favourite treat.
- Most dogs will learn the "Shake" trick quite quickly, and very soon, once you put out your hand, your dog will immediately lift their

paw and put it into your hand, without your assistance or any verbal cue.

Practice every day until they are 100% reliable with this trick, and then it will be time to add another trick to their repertoire.

TIP ***Most dogs are naturally either right or left pawed. If you know which paw your dog favours, ask them to shake this paw.***

ROLL OVER:

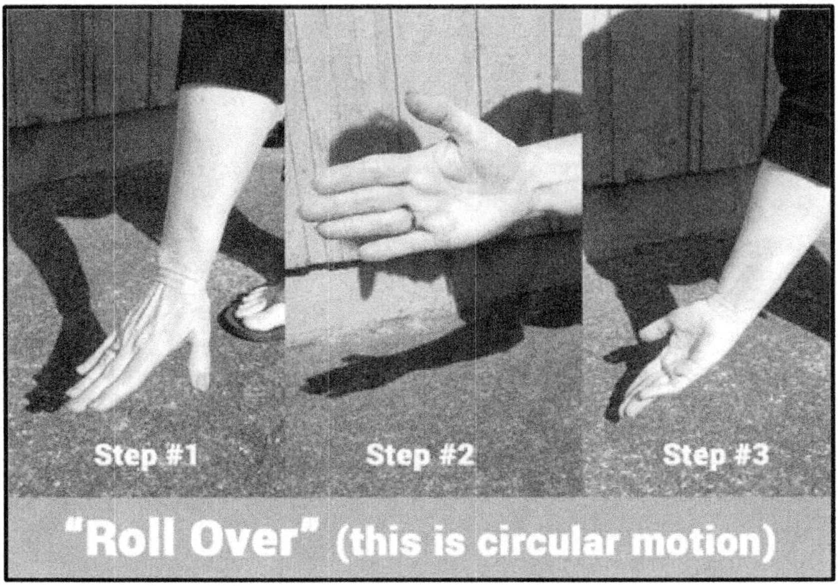

You will find that just as your dog is naturally either right or left pawed, they will also naturally want to roll either to the right or the left side. Take advantage of this by asking your dog to roll to the side they naturally prefer.

- Sit with your dog on the floor and put them in a lie down position.
- Hold a treat in your hand and place it close to their nose without allowing them to grab it.
- While they are in the lying position, move the treat to the right or left side of their head (the nose will follow the treat), so that they have to roll over to get to it.
- You will very quickly see which side they want to naturally roll to, and once you see this, move the treat to this side.

- When they roll over to this side, immediately give them the treat and praise them.
- You can say the verbal cue "Over" while you demonstrate the hand signal motion (moving your right hand in a circular motion) or moving the treat from one side of their head to the other with a half circle motion.

SIT PRETTY:

While this trick is a little more complicated, and most dogs pick up on it very quickly, remember that every dog is different so always exercise patience.

- Find a quiet space with few distractions and sit or stand in front of your dog and ask them to "Sit".
- Have a treat nearby (on a countertop or table) and when they sit, use both of your hands to lift up their front paws into the sitting pretty position, while saying the command "Sit Pretty".
- Help them balance in this position, while you praise them and give them the treat.
- Once your dog can perform the balancing part of the trick quite easily without your help, sit or stand in front of your dog while asking them to "Sit Pretty".

- Holding the treat above their head at the level of their nose would be when they sit pretty.
- If they attempt to stand on their back legs to get the treat, you may be holding the treat too high, which will encourage them to stand on their back legs to reach it. Go back to the first step and put them back into the "Sit" position and again lift their paws while their backside remains on the floor.
- After they learn the trick on verbal command, try saying the verbal cue while demonstrating the hand signal: holding your straight arm, fully extended, over your dog's head with a closed fist (pictured).
- Make this a fun and entertaining time for both of you and practice a few times every day until they can "Sit Pretty" on hand signal command every time you ask.

A smart young puppy should be able to easily learn these basic tricks before they are six months old and when you are patient and make your training sessions short and fun for your dog, they will be eager to learn so much more.

Crate Training

The best method for housetraining your dog is called crate training. Basically, you give your puppy many opportunities to do his or her business outside, so they are not tempted to do it inside.

During times when you cannot keep a constant watch on your puppy (such as when you're making dinner or sleeping), you put him or her in their crate as this will help to prevent hidden accidents elsewhere in your house. As long as you use the crate for this purpose and you help your puppy form a positive association with the crate, he or she will not mind being in it. Just do not use it as a form of punishment!

So, how exactly do you go about house training your puppy? Here's a step-by-step guide:

1. Choose a certain part of your yard where you want your dog to go.
2. Take your puppy outside every hour or so -- directly to the chosen spot every time.
3. When you take your puppy out, say "Go pee" as soon as you set him or her down in that area.
4. Wait for your puppy to do his business – and the moment they do, immediately praise them in an excited voice and give a small treat as a reward.
5. If your puppy does not have to go, take them back inside instead of letting him wander around.
6. When you're at home, keep a close eye on your puppy and confine them to whatever room you are in.
7. Watch your dog for signs that he or she has to go and take them outside immediately if they start to sniff the ground, walk in circles, or squat.
8. During times when you cannot physically watch your puppy, put him or her in their crate to reduce the risk of an accident – do not keep any food or water in the crate with them.
9. Let your puppy go outside to relieve his or herself immediately before putting them in the crate and also immediately after releasing them. You should also take your puppy outside shortly after a meal or when they wake up from a nap.
10. Take away your puppy's food and water about an hour before bedtime until they are able to go the whole night without an accident.

When you first bring your puppy home, you shouldn't expect him or her to be able to hold their bladder or bowels for more than an hour or two. Even so, you should start crate training right away so they learn good habits from an early age. As they get older, they will be able to wait longer before needing a bathroom break – about one hour for each month of age.

Adult Training

The Staffordshire is a dog that will thrive so long as they are getting to spend fun time and activities close to their human. Therefore, in order to ensure a happy and healthy dog that will not develop behaviour issues out of boredom or laziness, make sure that you get your dog involved in interesting activities, such as Advanced Obedience, Trick Training, Agility, Flyball or perhaps Barn Hunt.

When your dog is a full-grown adult (approximately two years of age), you will definitely want to begin more complicated or advanced training sessions.

When you have the desire and patience, you may be surprised at how many commands, tricks, routines or canine sports you can teach a happy, willing Staffy who trusts and respects their human guardian.

For instance, you may wish to teach your adult dog more advanced tricks, such as opposite sided paw shakes or rollovers, which are more difficult than you might expect and which this athletic dog is definitely capable of learning.

If you and your dog are really enjoying learning new tricks or routines together, consider teaching them a series of hand signals, such as "*Commando crawl*", "*Speak*" or "*Jump through the human hoop*", or perhaps get them certified as a therapy dog so they can brighten the days of those who must spend time in hospitals and care facilities.

Teaching your dog tricks and routines builds trust and respect, is fun for both of you, and a healthy way to exercise both your dog's mind and body, which will result in a happy, contented and well-behaved companion.

Over-Exercising

Be especially careful about over-exercising your fur friend when it's warm out because like humans, dogs can also collapse from heat stroke. Also, don't over-exercise when they are really young (as their muscles and bones are not yet fully developed).

Playtime

Every dog needs some down time or regular playtime each day, and while every dog will be different with respect to what types of games they may enjoy, most will really love any game involving retrieving a ball or soft toy. This will be a favourite pastime for the JRT, because they quickly become passionate about chasing fast-moving objects.

The loyal and smart Staffy may also be a very excited participant in a fun game of *"Search"*, where you ask your dog to *"Sit/Stay"* while you hide a favourite treat that they then have to use their nose to find.

To begin teaching the "Search" game, first time ask your dog to sit/stay while you slowly back away and place a treat where they can actually still see it. Return to where they are in their sit/stay and say, "OK! Search!" and point to where you just placed the treat. Each time you play this game, you can place the treat farther and farther away and then completely out of their sight before you release them to "Search!"

After a disciplined walk with your dog, a well-socialised Terrier will also enjoy being given the opportunity for some off-leash freedom to really stretch out by running free to play with other similar-sized dogs at the local dog park.

In a Nutshell

Taking the time to teach your dog basic rules and boundaries plus simple or complex tricks and interesting tasks and routines or sports to keep their mind engaged, will keep them both mentally and physically healthy and happy and you will raise a well-behaved dog that is a joy to be around.

While the robust Staffordshire can appear to have a stubborn streak or be strong-willed, if you provide this dog with consistently confident and firm direction, he or she will be a friendly and gentle family companion, with a loyal, loving personality that is willing to learn.

In order to ensure a healthy, happy and contented dog that is not overweight and will not develop behaviour issues out of boredom or neglect, you must take the time to involve them in daily moderate to high physical and mental exercise that can include different activities or routines where they get to burn off energy and develop their unique skills.

Chapter 13: What If You Slip Up?

"Dogs got personality.
Personality goes a long way."
— Quentin Tarantino

All the information, suggestions, tips and advice given in this book is the result of more than 40 years experience helping humans positively and effectively interact with the canine world.

If you take all that is written on these pages to heart, and regularly and consistently apply them, your dog will grow up to be a happy family member that will not have to suffer from any behavioural issues.

However, if your lifestyle drastically changes, you forget to exercise your dog or keep on top of basic or advanced training, let your dog take over, or you slip up for any number of reasons, problems may inevitably occur.

For instance, you may end up becoming too busy or distracted with your human life to provide your canine companion with what he or she needs on a daily basis to be a happy and fulfilled member of your family.

Realistically, there may be any number of other reasons why you may not consistently apply the information given here, and the following is an outline of just a few of the more common behavioural issues that could occur, with some tips that may help you get back on track.

When reading the following pages, please keep in mind that a specific behavioural problem is usually the result of many different possibilities or circumstances that have taken place between the human individual or family and the particular dog.

This means that properly addressing a specific unwanted behaviour often needs the assistance of a professional with a personal approach, who can ask the right questions to determine how the unwanted behaviour occurred, because it's often not what you may have initially thought.

Therefore, to generically outline possible ways that could possibly reverse an unwanted behaviour will be a guessing game, because without knowing the circumstances of the guardian and their family, and understanding the situation that triggered the unwanted behaviour, I can only make my best guess based on previous experience with similar problems.

As an example, there might be many reasons why the dog in question is, for instance, chewing the tassels on your precious Persian rug. As an example, this could be because they:

- are hungry
- are teething
- have a taste for wool
- think the tassels are a toy
- are a super high energy dog
- are left alone and are frustrated
- haven't been given appropriate toys to chew
- have not been taught rules and what is appropriate
- need a guardian with stronger leadership energy
- are bored and under-exercised
- are over-stimulated

As you can imagine, because there are endless dog and human combinations, it's possible for almost endless scenarios and reasons why a dog may develop a particular behavioural issue.

Therefore, please understand that without close observation and much more information explaining a particular situation, the following few common behavioural problems and the suggestions for alleviating them, will be my best guess.

Chewing Inappropriate Items
[Re-visit "*Distraction and Replacement*" in Chapter 10]

If your puppy or dog is chewing the carpet, your fingers, the legs of the coffee table, your shoes, or any other inappropriate item(s) that are not dog toys, rather than getting upset with your dog, you need to train yourself to be much more vigilant, and then distract and replace.

First make sure that all the chewing is not just because the puppy is teething. Have compassion because teething is painful for the puppy and they must chew to help alleviate the pain while those adult teeth are growing in.

Always make sure your puppy has plenty of chew toys and to help with the teething pain, give your puppy an old T-towel soaked in water, tied in knots and frozen in the freezer as a chew toy.

When your dog is a little older, already has pushed through their adult set of teeth and has decided, for instance, that the legs on your coffee table are good chew toys, it is possible that you:

- are not paying attention and taking the time to make sure your dog receives enough vigorous daily exercise, and/or,
- are not teaching your dog what is, and what is not appropriate for chewing by saying a firm and convincing "No", replacing the table leg with a toy they are allowed to chew, and praising them when they've got the right thing between their teeth.

Being Fearful of Loud Noises
[Re-visit *"Fear of Loud Noises"* in Chapter 10]

If you have raised a dog that has a fear of loud, popping noises, perhaps you haven't taken the time to read this information and apply the suggestions outlined, so read it now and practice until your dog loses or at least diminishes their fear.

Excessive Excitement When Friends Visit

[Re-visit *"Chapter 3: Overview of the Happy Staffordshire Bull Terrier"* and *"Chapter 12: Training Basics for a Happy Staffordshire Bull Terrier"*]

Make sure that you begin to teach an excitable young dog to be a calm follower as soon as you bring him or her home.

Always ignore an excited dog and do not touch or speak to them until they are calm and relaxed, otherwise you will inadvertently teach them that it is acceptable behaviour for them to be excited every time they see a human.

If they are overly excited when friends come to visit, stand between your dog and your friends, and create some space by pointing away and firmly telling your dog, "*GO*", and also ask your friends to ignore him or her.

Also, if you've been properly training your puppy or dog, you will have taught them to *"Sit"* on command, and a sitting dog is much more relaxed and easier to control.

Acting Aggressively on a Walk

[Re-visit *"Chapter 12: Training Basics for a Happy Staffordshire Bull Terrier"*]

Make sure that your dog is walking at your side without pulling on the leash when you are out for a walk.

When you train your dog to walk beside you, this *"tells"* them that YOU are their leader and in charge of every situation, which means they will be much less likely to act out or attempt to "protect" you from outside stimuli. If they DO try, immediately give a sharp tug on that Martingale collar along with a strong "***NO!***" to remind them who is the boss.

Pulling When on Leash

[Re-visit "*The Martingale Collar*" in Chapter 10]

If your dog is pulling on leash, chances are high that he or she is not wearing the proper training collar and you may not have taken the time to teach them to quietly walk at your side.

Buy your dog a Martingale collar, properly adjust it, and then the next time they try to pull ahead of you, give a sharp snap to this collar (toward yourself) and firmly say the word "***Heel***".

Repeating this process until your dog understands can take a few minutes or even several days, as each dog is different – be consistent and persistent until your dog gets it.

Also, turning circles or figure eights and changing directions suddenly when on a leash walk will quickly help to teach your dog their proper walking position, because if they are ahead of you, they are going to be stepped on or walked into.

<u>Stealing Food or Raiding the Garbage Can</u>
[Re-visit "*Ideal Living Conditions for a Happy Staffordshire Bull Terrier*" in Chapter 6]

Make sure you absolutely understand that the Staffordshire may be a highly food motivated breed. This is a muscular, agile and athletic dog will have no difficulty jumping up on counter tops. If given the opportunity and the food is enticing enough, any dog will steal food. This means that in order to avoid this possibility, you must be a vigilant guardian and make sure that you never leave any food they should not eat unattended or where they can reach it.

<u>Not Obeying Commands</u>
[Re-visit "*Chapter 12: Training Basics for a Happy Staffordshire Bull Terrier*"]

A well-trained Staffy is one that obeys the basic "*Come/Sit/Stay*" commands. If your dog is not obeying your commands, you may not have taken the time to properly train them, or you may have energy that is too weak for them to respect you as a leader. This dog needs a strong leader, and without it he or she may take a stubborn, dominant attitude, while they ignore you and then soon become your leader.

Get to work right away, step up your energy to ensure you are a strong enough leader, and train your dog so that everyone will be happy.

TIP ***We all have our off days, so don't get down on yourself if you occasionally slip up and are not being as vigilant, strong and confident a leader as you need to be with this dog.***

<u>In a Nutshell</u>

We humans will always have days when we are not as vigilant as we need to be, which means that we will inevitably "slip up" sometimes when raising our fur friends.

What you need to remember is that it's not the end of the world, because there is always a solution, and often simply re-reading the relevant chapters in this book can quickly and easily get you back on track to raising a happy and well-behaved Staffordshire that is a pleasure to be around.

Also, know that the familiar expression *"You can't teach an old dog new tricks"* is totally false. It doesn't matter what age a particular dog may be, because with patience and the right energy and knowledge, you absolutely CAN teach a dog of any age new tricks. It's us humans that have difficulties learning new tricks.

Chapter 14: Surprise Bonus Chapter

"Dogs have a way of finding the people who need them, and filling an emptiness we didn't ever know we had."
— Thom Jones

If you thought that the end of this book was in sight, well surprise, not quite yet, as I'd like to leave you with some canine wisdom and a short, funny, true story.

Happy Staffordshire Bull Terrier Question and Answer section

The following Q&A section is written from the dog's perspective, and although you may find it amusing, there are also valuable human lessons to be learned for anyone paying attention.

First, let me set the scene for the following situations:

This is a young, busy family, consisting of Mom and Dad, who work at home, one 12-year-old girl, and one 14-year-old boy, who share their lives with a neutered, 2-year-old dog named Harvey. They all live together in a large house with a medium-sized, fenced yard out the back.

The following questions, asked by various members of the family, are directed to the dog, and answered by the dog, as if our dogs could actually talk like their humans.

Each question the dog answers is followed by a short synopsis of the "lesson" we humans can learn from these various interactions.

Mom: **"Oh No! Why did you pee on the floor?"**

Harvey: *"I'm sorry, I didn't mean to, but you forgot to let me out before everyone left for that soccer game, and I just couldn't hold it any longer."*

Lesson: Humans often lead very busy and distracted lives, and in order to ensure their dog remains happy, they still need to always pay attention, which often means putting their canine friend's needs ahead of their own.

Girl: **"Yuckeeee! Harvey, why do you smell like dog poo?"**

Harvey: *"I was digging a hole in the back yard, and I guess those piles of doggy doo that the boy hadn't picked up yet got in the way."*

Lesson: Humans with convenient back yard doggy bathrooms often forget to be vigilant about picking up the yard. This is not only a smelly bad habit that busy (or lazy) guardians can be guilty of, it's also a considerable health hazard that attracts rats.

Boy: **"What's wrong, Harvey? You like to fetch — go get that ball!"**

Harvey: *"Yes, I like to fetch, but it's hot out here, I'm getting exhausted and if I don't get water soon, I may pass out."*

Lesson: Sometimes we humans sharing our lives with dogs that have great stamina and love to fetch tend to forget that the temperature of the day, that doesn't seem extreme to us, can quickly be too much for a dog that is running back and forth fetching a ball while we're standing still.

We also forget that many dogs, despite their discomfort, have a strong desire to retrieve and like to please their humans so much that they may continue to fetch that ball even though they may be about to collapse from heat exhaustion and are dying of thirst.

Dad: **"What happened in here, Harvey! You've made a huge mess of all these boxes I had neatly stacked in the carport! What's wrong with you?"**

Harvey: *"I saw a squirrel in here eating through the boxes and I was just trying to protect the home. I finally got rid of him, and he won't be coming back. Sorry I knocked over the boxes."*

Lesson: Often we tend to quickly blame our canine friends when a mess is created for which there seems to be no explanation. We need to first think beyond simply blaming the dog for unexplained disarray, as there is often a good explanation that, in most cases, exonerates your canine companion.

Mom: **"Harvey! What have you done? I left a plate of cheese and crackers on the coffee table for our guests. Did you eat them?"**

Harvey: *"I smelled them when I was passing through and couldn't resist. I love cheese and the crackers were OK too, but now I think I might have to throw up."*

Lesson: Many of our canine companions (such as the Staffordshire) don't know when to stop when it comes to filling their stomach. Therefore, if you have one of these dogs with an endless appetite for anything remotely resembling food, you need to be vigilant about never leaving human food, garbage or anything edible where they can reach it.

Boy: **"You bad, bad dog, Harvey! You've chewed the laces off my expensive tennis shoes."**

Harvey: *"But they smell just the same as those old shoes you gave me to play with, and now you're mad at me? I'm confused."*

***Lesson**:* Think about what you allow your canine friend to play with, because giving them old discarded shoes, socks or other articles of clothing, etc., to play with can easily cause confusion in the canine mind when you get mad if they decide to chew your new shoes.

Girl: **"You're covering my bed in mud Harvey! Get out!"**

Harvey: *"But I like being next to you, and you let me sleep on your bed when I was a puppy, so please let me up."*

Lesson: If you'd rather not share your bed with a dog that could have just walked through a muddy puddle or killed a rat in the back yard, don't make the mistake of allowing them to sleep with you when they're a cute and much smaller puppy. If you do, it's unfair to blame your canine companion for wanting to continue this habit that you literally taught them.

Dad: **"Are you kidding me, Harvey? Where's the burgers I left on the picnic table for our guests!"**

Harvey: *"There were circling crows and I tried to chase them away, but they smelled so good that I couldn't resist. I'm sorry – I ate them while you were getting a beer. They were so delicious - got any more?"*

Lesson: Dogs are carnivorous and no matter their size, whether a tiny Chihuahua, a large Mastiff, or an agile and muscular Staffordshire Bull Terrier, if given the opportunity, their desire to eat meat is a strong instinct they cannot ignore. If you leave meat unattended, and your dog eats it, don't blame your canine companion.

Moral of the Q&A section

Always DO pay attention to what your dog is trying to tell you, because (in addition to the above), there are so many other lessons we humans can learn from our beloved canine companions. Watching out and learning these lessons and appropriately acting upon them, will help you to raise a Happy Staffordshire that will never have to experience unwanted behaviours.

There are so many lessons we humans can learn from our beloved canine companions IF we are paying attention.

Happy Staffordshire Bull Terrier True Story

Before we close this Chapter, I hope you will enjoy the following true short story:

Ozzy's New Tiles

I was dog-sitting Ozzy, the Staffordshire Bull Terrier, for clients of mine who had just recently installed a new tile entranceway in their home where previously there had been carpet tiles. The owners warned me that they were having a *"little problem"* getting Ozzy used to the new, shiny and quite slippery tiles and I told them not to worry about it, as I presumed this was a minor issue.

However, I soon found out that the joke was on me, because once I had delivered Ozzy's owners to the airport and I returned to the home with Ozzy on leash at my side, I was brought to an abrupt halt when I opened the door and Ozzy refused to enter the house.

Ozzy stopped so suddenly that all the groceries I was carrying became airborne and ended up strewn across the floor while it felt like I had become attached to a wriggling fire hydrant. OK, so much for the *"little"* problem Ozzy was having with the new flooring because he flatly refused to put even one paw on those shiny new tiles.

Thank goodness it was a pleasant summer day because now was the time to start working out Ozzy's fear of shiny surfaces and this meant keeping the front door open.

I tied Ozzy's leash to the railing near the door, rescued my groceries from the tiled floor, found some of Ozzy's favourite treats, and returned to untie Ozzy while I showed him I had something he wanted. He was immediately interested in the treats and started to follow me into the house only to abruptly stop at the edge of the tiles.

I went inside a couple of feet and sat down with his treats on the tiled surface, holding my hand out to offer him one. He stretched as far as he could without stepping on the tiles trying to get to the treats he really wanted, while I kept calmly encouraging him to move forward.

Finally, after several failed attempts to get him to put even one paw on the dreaded tile surface, he completely flattened himself onto his belly and used his legs like a frog to *"swim"* his way across the tiles to get the treats I was offering.

This was definitely one of the funniest things I had ever seen a dog do, but I had to be careful not to laugh because he needed me to be his strong and confident leader, so I stifled my laughter and praised him for being so brave and figuring out how to get his treat.

So now here was Ozzy flat on his belly in the middle of the shiny tile surface with his beloved carpeting about ten slippery tiles away. I stood up and moved farther into the house onto the carpeted area, still encouraging him to come and get his favourite treats.

He stared at me with those pleading eyes that seemed to say *"help me out of this predicament",* and all I could do was talk softly and confidently to him, pretending everything was just fine as I asked him to come and get another treat.

After a couple of minutes, Ozzy decided that the only way to get what he wanted was to *"swim"* a little farther and he flailed with his front paws and kicked with his back feet like a frog until he made his way onto the carpet, where he immediately bounded into life.

Stifling my laughter, I immediately praised and petted him, gave him several of his favourite treats, and all was now right in Ozzy's world, until it came time to go out for a lunchtime walk around the block.

I hitched up Ozzy's leash to his Martingale collar and started to walk toward the front door, which involved crossing over the tiled entranceway, hoping he would forget about his fear, but as soon as we reached the edge of the carpet, he immediately put the brakes on.

I stopped with him, keeping some forward tension on his leash, as I offered him a treat if he would just take one step onto the tiles. Instead, he immediately dropped onto his belly again, like a penguin about to slide down a snow bank, and started pushing himself across the tiles to get to the treat I was offering.

Such a sight he was and so determined to get his treat without having to walk – you had to give him credit for his amazing ingenuity.

When he got to my outstretched hand and gobbled down his treat, I gently picked him up and placed his feet onto the dreaded tiles and again encouraged him to walk toward me. This time, although he remained crouched low, he gingerly attempted his first step, and then another and another until you could actually see a light bulb go off in his doggy brain when he realized that the smooth surface of the tiles was indeed safe to walk on.

I happily praised him for his bravery and gave him another treat, and then a few more times in and out the door and although he would slightly hesitate when stepping onto the tiles, and stoop down to sniff them, within three days of practicing our little routine, the dreaded slippery tile flooring was no longer a problem for this smart and determined Terrier.

When his owners returned from their holiday, you can imagine how happy they were to know that they no longer had to carry a 32-pound (14.5 kg) Ozzy across their entranceway.

Lesson to learn: ***No matter the age of your dog, and how much you may have socialised them, when you change something in their world, they can become nervous, confused and traumatized. The only way to work through this is with much patience and understanding, coupled with persistent calm energy, and of course, favourite treats.***

Chapter 15: Conclusion and Reviews

"Once you have a wonderful dog,
a life without one is a life diminished."
— Dean Koontz

This book is written to help anyone thinking of sharing their life with the energetic, fearless and loving Staffordshire Bull Terrier, to first understand whether or not they truly have the time, energy and lifestyle that would be compatible with raising a healthy and happy dog.

Once it's been decided that this tireless canine is the right breed to share your life with, the purpose of this book is to help you understand how to properly care for them.

This will include socialising, training and providing this dog with adequate physical and mental daily exercise, the best food, regular grooming and a safe environment, so that this dog can live the longest and most contented life possible.

There are already plenty of books written, and many different trainers and opinions concerning how to correct a dog that may be suffering from any number of behavioural issues.

However, to my knowledge, there are no breed-specific books that take the time to outline how most issues that could have been avoided, may have instead been inadvertently created by the dog's human guardian. Therefore, this breed-specific book stands out from all other current publications, because it highlights that almost all problems, both mentally and physically, may occur as a result of:

- lack of knowledge
- lack of experience
- minimal research
- being unaware of how much time is involved in raising their chosen dog
- energy incompatibility
- lifestyle incompatibility

Further, this book describes in detail what the human guardian needs to understand and commit to doing on a daily basis in order to ensure that this dog's needs are met, so that they can raise a happy, healthy and well-behaved companion that never has to experience behavioural issues.

There is much knowledge contained within the pages of this book that has been gained over some 40 years working with dogs. This information will help anyone serious about raising a ***HAPPY*** Staffordshire Bull Terrier, so that they can easily implement all the practical tips of this book without having to hire a professional to help them correct any sort of future behavioural problems.

In a nutshell, this book will help you determine if you are the right match for this robust breed, and contains all you need to raise a Happy Staffordshire that will never have to experience unwanted behaviours or end up behind bars at the local SPCA.

What Past Clients Have to Say

The following are a few happy reviews from some of my past dog whispering clients, who did the work required to turn their chosen fur friend into a happy and well-behaved companion.

I have taught these clients how to apply some of the tips and techniques described in this book (such as how to establish yourself as the pack leader) and they easily managed to get back on track to raising a happy and well-behaved companion.

Thus, rather than taking my word for the effectiveness of the methods contained in this book, perhaps you would prefer to hear from some of my happy clients.

> "*Thank you for your report and teaching me to be a pack leader ... this has worked remarkably as Drew and Sammy have responded well beyond my expectations... Drew is very calm and relaxed and our walks are now very enjoyable...*
>
> *I want you to know that I really appreciate your help... Results have been spectacular and both dogs have evolved into superheroes and have accepted me as their pack leader and respond positively...*"
> ~ Klaus, Drew, Sammy & Max the Cat
>
> "*I just wanted to thank you again for our lesson today. You really are amazing with dogs. Tim and I learned so much from you, it's really neat to see the difference it makes in the dogs when you take control...*"
> ~ Morgan, Tim, Grizzly, Bella & Bear
>
> *"I was at the point I was ready to give Jake away because I was so concerned about how he reacted every time someone came to the door. It was really embarrassing! Honestly, within three hours of Asia being here, Jake was a different dog. We learned how to become the pack leader and control him..."*
> ~ Sharon, Mike & Jake

"My partner and I and our dog Rollo recently moved to Victoria from up north. Rollo, unused to city life and walking on a leash, was nervous and reactive around other dogs. Asia showed us how we need to behave so he could relax. After just one session the difference was very impressive – walks have become relaxing and enjoyable again – for all of us…"
~ Tim, Mary & Rollo

"Thank you for helping me become the guardian that Ida needs. She was a good dog to start with, now she is an incredible dog. She walks well on lead, stays in my unfenced yard, and comes when called. I am often complimented on what a well-behaved dog I have. Thanks for making it all happen..."
~ Kristiane & Ida

Published by Worldwide Information Publishing 2021

Disclaimer and Legal Notice: This product is not legal or medical advice and should not be interpreted in that manner. You need to do your own due-diligence to determine if the content of this product is right for you. The authors and the affiliates of this product are not liable for any damages or losses associated with the content in this product.

While every attempt has been made to verify the information shared in this publication, neither the author nor the affiliates assume any responsibility for errors, omissions or contrary interpretation of the subject matter herein. Any perceived slights to any specific person(s) or organization(s) are purely unintentional. We have no control over the nature, content and availability of the web sites listed in this book.

The accuracy and completeness of information provided herein and opinions stated herein are not guaranteed or warranted to produce any particular results, and the advice and strategies, contained herein may not be suitable for every individual. The authors shall not be liable for any loss incurred as a consequence of the use and application, directly or indirectly, of any information presented in this work. This publication is designed to provide information in regard to the subject matter covered.

The information included in this book has been compiled to give an overview of the subject and detail some of the symptoms, treatments etc. that are available. It is not intended to give medical advice. For a firm diagnosis of any health condition, and for a treatment plan suitable for you and your dog, you should consult your veterinarian or consultant.

The writers of this book and the publisher are not responsible for any damages or negative consequences that may arise as a result of following any of the treatments or methods highlighted in this book.

Printed in Great Britain
by Amazon

68162618R00112